knives cooks love

knives cooks love

SELECTION. CARE. TECHNIQUES. RECIPES.

sur la table with **sarah jay**

FOREWORD BY CHEF EMERIL LAGASSE

PHOTOGRAPHY BY BEN FINK

Andrews McMeel
Publishing, LLC

Kansas City

other books by sur la table

Things Cooks Love

The Art and Soul of Baking

08 09 10 11 12 TWP 10 9 8 7 6 5 4 3 2 1

LIBRARY OF CONGRESS CATALOGING-IN-PUBLICATION DATA:

Knives cooks love : selection, care, techniques / Sur La Table, with Sarah Jay.—1st ed.
    p. cm.
 ISBN-13: 978-0-7407-7002-9
 ISBN-10: 0-7407-7002-0
 1. Knives. 2. Cutting. I. Jay, Sarah. II. Sur La Table (Firm)
 TX657.K54K65 2008
 621.9'32—dc22

                            2008007350

www.andrewsmcmeel.com

www.surlatable.com

Design: Vertigo Design NYC

Food Stylist: Susan Spungen

Prop Stylist: Roy Finamore

To all cooks who truly value their cutlery

contents

Acknowledgments

WHEN WE THOUGHT OF WHAT TOOL was the most indispensible tool in the kitchen, there was only one choice: the knife. Without it, most cooks could not proceed with even the simplest dish. We knew we wanted an experienced researcher and writer for this book, someone who could distill a vast amount of information down to its practical essence. That person was Sarah Jay, former executive editor of *Fine Cooking* magazine.

Without Jacob Maurer, knife buyer and aficionado extraordinaire, this book would not have happened. Working with Sarah, he guided us through the essential elements of the book and introduced us to some of the most amazing knife experts in the business. Ben Fink's masterful eye teamed up with Alison Lew, Roy Finamore, and Susan Spungen to make this a handsome and very inspired book.

Thanks to Nach Waxman for planting the seed for the book and to Kirsty Melville, Lane Butler, and Jean Lucas from Andrews McMeel for their guidance. Sur La Table staff members Rebecca Burgess, Nathan Slusser, Henry Kohout, and Robb Ginter all helped us accomplish our ultimate goal. Bill Dullaghan's unwavering support through the creation of three books in two years was invaluable.

Last but not least, thanks to our customers, whose passion for great knives has confirmed that creating this book was the essential next step in the Sur La Table publishing program.

—SUR LA TABLE

DOZENS OF PEOPLE HELPED this book come to fruition. Jacob Maurer eased me into the fascinating subject of knives, and I couldn't have had a better resource for all things knife related. I also leaned heavily on Bob Entin, whose enthusiasm for knives and generosity of time seem to know no bounds.

Many other experts graciously took time from their busy schedules, and I send a huge thank-you to Harold Arimoto, Scott Belovin, Jack Bevington, Dennis Epstein, Dan Freel, Sal Glesser, Brian Hayes, Mark Henry, Hiro Hirano, Norman Kornbluth, Bob Kramer, Robert Kufahl, Evan Lobel, Erik Ried, Holli Roberts, Charles Robertson, and Mike Staib.

I had a wonderful corps of recipe testers, too numerous to name here, who gave me honest feedback about what worked and what didn't. My appreciation also goes out to Mala Darrow, Kathy Blake, Lori Longbotham, Denitza Krasteva, Rich Pinto, and especially to Suha Jhaveri for her apple pinwheel brilliance.

I want to thank Martha Holmberg and Susie Middleton for being terrific bosses, Jennifer Armentrout for backstopping me at the last minute, Steve Hunter for sending me his gorgeous carbon steel knife, and Molly Stevens, Joanne Smart, Tony Rosenfeld, Maryellen Driscoll, and my colleagues at *Fine Cooking* magazine for just being there.

My friends Margot Weiss, Diana Pittet, and Dawn McMullan supported me both professionally and emotionally, and Kerry Sherck did that and more: she was my listening board and cooking partner, and she never once complained when dinner at seven turned out to be dinner at ten.

I'm indebted to Mary Hadar for her valuable editorial feedback at every stage of writing, and to Kim Masibay for throwing me a long lifeline at one crucial stage. From structural advice to wordsmithing, the two of them steered the manuscript toward the light of day.

Finally, let me just say for the record that I have the best mom in the entire world. She may not give a hoot about knives, but she was always there with an offer to help. I love you, Mom!

—SARAH JAY

Foreword by Chef Emeril Lagasse

ASK ANY COOK OR CHEF YOU MEET and I bet they'll say their knives are the most highly valued cooking tools in their possession. Cooks care about their knives like no other kitchen tool. They guard them closely and never leave them alone in a busy kitchen. They keep their knives safe by placing them in a knife block or carrying them in a knife roll to protect their vulnerable edges. They call on their knives to perform their duty many, many times throughout the course of a single day. When their knives are dull, cooks sharpen them so they'll regain their optimum edge. Cooks were taught to use knives properly, so they promptly wash and dry them after each use to prolong their lives and to keep them ready for action. Young cooks dream of owning that special knife or set of knives made by a highly respected knife manufacturer or craftsman.

All of this and so much more is true of cooks' knives, and yet, as my friend and master cutler Bill Muth once told me, other than the refrigerator, the stove, or perhaps the can opener, the knife is often the least discussed tool in the kitchen. How is it that we've come to take our most primal, basic tool for granted? Perhaps it is because knives have been around for so long; they are such an integral part of the kitchen that we do not question their worth or contemplate their history. But when we take a moment to reflect on these things, we see a vast world open up to us and we ask ourselves, how would we have gotten here without them?

I remember one particular day that changed the way I think about knives. During one of my first meetings with the folks from the prestigious Wüsthof knife factory, I was taken to a knife museum in their hometown of Solingen, Germany. It was on that visit that I realized knives had an incredible history worth studying and getting involved in.

Our forefathers used the simplest, most rudimentary type of knife, a sharp stone, to bring food to their tables and to protect themselves against their enemies. As both civilization and technology progressed, knives became manufactured tools made from different materials and formulated in different shapes and sizes for varying purposes. Today, the knife is predominantly a kitchen tool, and, although many folks may proudly possess nice kitchen equipment, knives included, they have little or no knowledge about how to properly care for or sharpen a knife.

That's where this book comes in. In the most studious of manners, but using simple, easy-to-understand language, author Sarah Jay demystifies the knife for us all. Look inside and discover the world of the tool that provides a comfort zone in the kitchen: the knife, the truest symbol of the culinary edge.

WHEN YOU WERE LITTLE, someone showed you how to tie your shoes and hold a pencil, and then later, how to ride a bicycle and drive a car. Maybe, if you were lucky, someone also showed you how to cook. But unless you've gone to culinary school, there's one life skill that you've probably never been taught, and that's how to use a knife.

It's kind of surprising when you think about it. Our knives are the most fundamental tool in the kitchen, and yet we're left pretty much on our own to figure out how to handle them. The problem is, most of us haven't figured it out. We make do the best we can and, sure, we get by. But if you're the kind of person who cooks for the pure joy of it, then "getting by" just doesn't cut it.

We tend to think of cooking as standing at the stove, pushing around the contents of a sauté pan, but the truth is, most of our active cooking is spent over by the cutting board, trimming and paring and slicing and dicing. So why shouldn't we invest a little energy into making our chopping time more efficient and enjoyable? That means buying decent knives, learning how to use them, and knowing how to take care of them. It's worth it—no other piece of kitchen equipment has the capacity to make cooking so much fun. If you've never cut with a knife that's incredibly sharp and perfectly balanced, that feels almost like an extension of your hand, then you're missing out on one of cooking's greatest pleasures.

Deep down inside, we want to feel great about our knives. After all, we love our Dutch oven, our stand mixer, and our mortar and pestle, and we use those items only occasionally. Yet many of us don't feel that much affection for our knives, even though we reach for them many times a day. Perhaps the knives we own are mediocre, or we're using the wrong knife at the wrong time, or we don't know how or are afraid to keep them sharp. Or maybe it's just that we don't have very good knife skills, so we're diffident or disorganized with our chopping.

If any of those things are holding you back, that's about to change. Knives aren't mysterious objects, and they aren't all that difficult to use well. The only reason that we don't feel as comfortable with them as we might is that we've never had a guide to show us the way.

This book will be your guide. You can read it from start to finish, or you can parachute into any chapter to retrieve the specific bit of information you want. If you're ready to upgrade to better knives, head straight to chapter 3 for shopping tips. If you're mystified by sharpening (and who isn't?), check out chapter 4 for help in choosing a method

introduction

that's quick and foolproof. If you want to master specific culinary cuts, skip right over to part II, where you'll discover a neat technique for coring peppers and a new way to slice onions, plus some practical tips that apply to all your chopping. This book also offers a few useful nuggets that you won't encounter anywhere else. You'll learn how to decode the function of any knife just by looking at its shape (page 19). You'll find a "three-plus-three" strategy for customizing your own twelve-piece knife set (page 51). And you'll get a comparison chart that clearly explains honing and sharpening, so you can finally understand when to do one or the other (page 57).

With knowledge comes confidence. When you have a nice sharp knife in hand, along with the skills to use it, you'll feel more empowered in the kitchen. You'll be poised to take on any dish, no matter how long the prep list. You'll cook more, and you'll cook better. So the time has come. Take a deep breath, relax, and let's get started.

a primer on knives

PART ONE

BEFORE WE CAN TALK about how a knife is made, we need to understand what it's made of. And that story started hundreds of thousands of years ago, when early humans discovered that some types of stones cut better than others. Ever since, we've been on a quest to find the ideal material for our blades, moving from flint, obsidian, shells, and slate to metals like copper, bronze, and raw iron. None of them was perfect. They were either too hard, too soft, too brittle, or too difficult to sharpen.

Then, about three thousand years ago, our ancestors invented steel (it probably appeared first in the Far East and then later in the Middle East), and finally we were on the way to a truly great knife. Created by adding a drop of carbon to iron, steel was hard—much harder than any metal that came before—and it could be honed to a fine edge.

the making of a knife

steel blades

INITIALLY, STEEL BLADES weren't crafted with cooking in mind. The priority was weaponry—swords, daggers, and the like—and these were primarily available only to those with affluence and power. For much of the Iron Age, most common folk were still tackling their everyday cutting tasks with primitive stone tools.

As the Iron Age gave way to the Roman Era and then the Middle Ages, from about A.D. 500 to 1500, steel knives gradually found their way into homes and kitchens. They were treasured possessions: Handles and sheaths were often elaborately decorated or carved, even if the blade itself was fairly unremarkable in design. Some specialized forms existed—medieval French cooks used a long-bladed slicing knife called a *minchoir*—but there were evidently few knives intended solely for preparing and eating food. Indeed, the medieval custom was to bring one's dagger to the dining table, where it was used for both eating and defending oneself at the occasional mealtime brawl. (In the early 1600s, Louis XIII of France decreed that personal knives could not be brought to the table; a rounded-tip blade was offered to diners instead, the progenitor of today's table knife.)

Throughout Europe, the knife-making trade was tightly intertwined with sword making and other weapons production up until the tenth and eleventh centuries, when an independent cutlery industry began to emerge. By the sixteenth and seventeenth centuries, knifemakers had set up shop throughout the continent, with a few regions, such as Sheffield, England, and Solingen, Germany, becoming centers of production as a result of their proximity to iron mines and waterways, which powered the iron-processing furnaces.

EVEN THOUGH STAINLESS-STEEL KNIVES do a fine job, some chefs are returning to old-fashioned carbon steel blades. Why? Simply this: They're super sharp and they seem to hold their sharpness for longer. And when carbon steel does start to dull, it's a lot easier to resharpen. With time and proper care, it will develop a patina that reduces its reactivity with acidic ingredients. If you like the tarnished look and don't mind a little extra maintenance—

carbon steel knives— poised for a comeback?

you need to be vigilant about drying to prevent rusting—consider a carbon steel knife. They're not widely available in cookware shops, so you'll need to poke around a little to find one. A tip: Seek out retailers that sell traditional Japanese knives or authentic French Sabatier knives.

The best knife I've ever owned is a carbon steel Sabatier bought in 1976 in France. It's ugly as sin. It discolors and rusts if you look at it the wrong way. It's actually a sole filleting knife but I use it for just about everything. I've never found a knife that I like half as much as that one.

—Steven Raichlen, author of *The Barbecue Bible*

By the early 1900s, cooking knives had diversified into numerous shapes and styles, but there hadn't been any truly significant advances in the material itself. Although steel-making technology had made strides, becoming more efficient and consistent, knives were always made of plain steel, what we now refer to as carbon steel. They were sharp and easy to use, but they had flaws. They rusted easily, they pitted and stained when exposed to acidic ingredients, and they were reactive, making delicate food like fish taste metallic.

the arrival of stainless steel

Then, in 1913, a breakthrough. A British research chemist named Harry Brearley added chromium to steel to see if it would make the metal harder. It did, and it also developed two new and intriguing traits: It didn't react with acid and it didn't rust. (The chromium had formed an invisible oxide coating on the surface of the metal, which inhibited corrosion.) Although others had apparently made this same discovery years earlier, Brearley was the first to see its potential for knives and to do something about it. He teamed up with a local cutler—he lived in Sheffield—and this novel metal alloy became known as stainless steel.

It took a few decades for stainless-steel knives to permeate the marketplace, but eventually, they could be found almost everywhere. They looked terrific—so shiny and pretty—and all that chromium made the blade very durable. But there was a little problem: They were a bear to sharpen and, even at their peak sharpness, they didn't perform that impressively. They simply couldn't take an edge as well as carbon steel knives. By mid century, professional cooks and butchers had returned to their old carbon steel blades, and the stainless-steel knife had acquired a bad reputation.

better alloys: getting the mix right

After the disappointment of those first stainless knives, steel producers got to work refining their product. From the 1950s right through to today, they've been searching for the holy grail of cutting steel, an alloy that would be very

KNIFEMAKERS DESCRIBE their stainless-steel knives in different ways, using terms like *stain-resistant* or *stain free* or *rust free* or just plain *stainless*—but in fact, no so-called stainless-steel knife is completely impervious to corrosion. Some are more rust resistant than others—the key variable is the amount of chromium in the steel—but any knife that's exposed to salt, acidity, or moisture for a long time will eventually discolor or rust (because salt

stainless isn't truly stainless

and acids erode the protective chromium oxide coating). But don't worry; as long as you take care of your knives by washing and drying them fairly soon after use, corrosion will likely never be an issue.

YOU DON'T REALLY NEED TO KNOW what vanadium and molybdenum do to steel, but you might be curious, since they're occasionally mentioned in knife-marketing blurbs. Here's a short list of some of the ingredients that go into the steel stockpot—it's a complicated brew because each element interplays with the others.

IRON The basic material for all types of steel.

CARBON An essential element that hardens steel, allowing it to take and hold a sharp edge. It also makes it more brittle and prone to rusting.

CHROMIUM Eleven percent or more chromium improves rust resistance and usually qualifies a knife as "stainless." It also improves durability.

metallurgy for dummies

MOLYBDENUM Increases hardness and rust resistance and reduces brittleness. Helps steel retain its strength and hardness during tempering. Used in most stain-resistant knives.

VANADIUM Enhances toughness, improving sharpness without making steel brittle. Helps resist wear.

MANGANESE Magnifies the benefits of carbon, increasing hardness and strength. Improves wear resistance.

TUNGSTEN Helps maintain hardness. Increases heat, wear, and shock resistance.

COBALT Enhances hardening while maintaining ease of sharpening.

NICKEL Adds toughness and possibly aids in corrosion resistance.

hard, sharp, durable (not brittle), stainless, and easy to sharpen.

Modern stainless-steel alloys are fabricated from a complex mix of elements, each one contributing a certain trait to the metal. In a way, the making of steel is a little like baking a cake. Most cakes contain sugar, flour, butter, and eggs, but knowing that doesn't tell you anything about the character of a cake: how coarse its crumb is, what it tastes like. What matters to the baker is the ratio of those ingredients, the mixing method, the baking time and temperature. Same goes for steel. All stainless-steel "recipes" start with iron, carbon, and chromium, plus maybe a splash of vanadium and molybdenum and a pinch of other elements. But it's the proportions, along with how they're mixed and cooked, that determines the nature of the steel.

To sell their knives, some brands reveal a few of the ingredients in their steel alloys,

what is "high-carbon" stainless steel?

while others don't refer to the steel at all. It doesn't matter either way. You'll never get the complete formula (they're guarded like state secrets), and even if you did, you wouldn't know what to make of it. In the end, all knifemakers are aiming for a blade that cuts and sharpens beautifully but that's also stain resistant and flexible. The problem is that those tend to be opposing traits—it's nearly impossible to achieve everything in a single knife. Some steels are very hard and durable but also quite challenging to sharpen. Others may take a razor edge but they won't hold it for long, so they'll need frequent honing. As a knife consumer, you don't need to get caught up in the details of specific types of steel, but you should be aware that all steels are not created equal.

steel-clad knives: the new (old) frontier

These days, Japan is producing the world's most technologically advanced steel, and the Japanese are also using these new metals in clever ways. Rather than limiting themselves to just one type of steel, some Japanese knifemakers are joining two different steels together in one blade. This approach, first developed centuries ago by Japanese samu-

rai swordsmiths, captures the best qualities of both steels.

Here's how it works: A layer of very sharp (but brittle) carbon steel is sandwiched between two or more layers of a flexible stainless steel. Sharpening the cutting edge exposes the middle layer of carbon steel, just as sharpening a pencil reveals the fragile graphite core, while the rest of the blade is protected by the softer steel. The result is a tough stainless blade that can take an exquisitely keen edge.

These "sandwiched" steel blades go by various names. If they're made using traditional forging techniques, they may be called *kasumi.* When contemporary methods are employed, you may hear the phrase *metal cladding,* or a Japanese term, *honwarikomi.*

how a blade is made

Knife retailers hear it constantly from their customers: "Is this knife stamped or forged?" Those two terms refer to the two main methods of blade manufacturing, and in the past, just knowing whether a knife was stamped or forged could tell you something about its quality: Forged was always better. But that's no longer true, and it's time to stop using this difference as a measure of excellence.

THE TERM "DAMASCUS" refers to two very different kinds of steel. One type, known as wootz Damascus, originated several centuries ago in the Middle East. The swords and knives made from this steel were legendary for their distinctive "watered" appearance and for their searing performance in battle; they combined extreme sharpness with toughness and flexibility. The specific technique for crafting these magnificent weapons disappeared for about two hundred years, though bladesmiths have recently uncovered the secrets.

The other type of Damascus, known as pattern welding, began as a way to create a more reliable steel (until the late nineteenth century, steel quality was frustratingly inconsistent). Bladesmiths found that by folding and twisting together a variety of different steels, they could achieve a tougher, sharper blade. The layering of dissimilar metals also produced a unique rippled

the beauty of damascus steel

pattern on each knife (it's not just on the surface; the layering penetrates the entire blade). This is the primary technique used to produce Damascus knives today. Now that commercial steelmaking has improved, the appeal of pattern Damascus is largely aesthetic—controlling and manipulating the pattern has become an art form—but some aficionados also feel that the layered grain makes the edge more "toothy," better at biting into food.

True pattern-welded Damascus knives are artisan products—hand crafted, quite costly, and not your average department store find. While many mass-produced knives feature a swirly pattern on the blade, these would be more accurately described as Damascus-style knives. The pattern is superficial; it doesn't penetrate the entire blade as it does with true Damascus. That's not to say that Damascus-style knives can't be good quality, but you should know there's a big difference.

Pattern-welded, handcrafted
Damascus knife by Bob Kramer

To make a knife, the metal is first formed into the rough shape of a blade, called a blank. Blanks for stamped knives are punched out from a thin sheet of steel, much as you stamp out dough with a cookie cutter.

Forged blanks, by contrast, are created from individual steel bricks, called billets, that are heated to thousands of degrees and then pounded into a basic blade form. Although some artisans still forge their knives by hand, commercial knifemakers today use huge industrial machines. The older-style machines use the drop-forging method, whereby massive hammers slam down onto the hot steel billet, compressing it into a blank. In cities like Solingen, Germany, you can feel the ground shake when these forges are operating. Drop-forging is becoming somewhat obsolete now that many major manufacturers have switched to a newer method, called precision forging. The steel billet enters the machine, but instead of being pounded into shape, it's squeezed between two rolling pins and compressed. Precision forging gives a more consistent product than drop-forging, and it's also more environmentally friendly. Both forging methods produce a relatively thick, solid knife with a knob of metal, called a bolster, between the

heel of the blade and the handle (see page 48 for photo).

According to conventional wisdom, forged knives are better than stamped for a few reasons: They're heavier and more durable, plus the process of heating and shaping the steel changes its molecular structure, making it even harder and potentially sharper. Stamped knives, the thinking goes, are inferior because of the thin, light blade and poor-quality steel.

Although those generalizations were once fairly accurate, things have changed a lot in recent years. First of all, stamped knives are now being laser cut from superior new steel alloys that have been heat treated, essentially altering their structure just as forging does. Second, the golden rule that heavy knives are better is no longer so golden. Many chefs and home cooks are finding a lot to love about a lighter knife. Not all stamped knives are terrific—it's still true that the bottom of the market is dominated by cheap stamped knives—but today, some of the best (and priciest) knives are cut from a thin sheet of metal rather than forged from a thick billet.

The forged versus stamped divide is helpful in one way, however. Forged knives are heavier, stamped knives are lighter, and most people find that they lean toward one style or the other.

All steel blades, whether forged or stamped, go through several more steps in their transition from blank to finished product. The blades are repeatedly blasted with heat and then quickly cooled. This heating and cooling process, called tempering, hardens the metal while developing its flexibility—in short, it toughens the steel. Tempering is a critical step, and how it's done can affect the quality of the knife. After tempering, the sides of the blade are ground, a handle is attached, and the edge is polished.

The classic European-style knife handle features two flat pieces of wood, called scales, that are triple-riveted to the blade extension, called the tang (see page 48 for photo). But you'll also find handles made of plastic, rubber, metal, compressed wood, or resin-infused wood, and they may sport ergonomic shapes or trendy colors. Depending on the material, the handle might be injection molded, welded, or riveted to the tang or else simply tapped on with a hammer (as with the traditional Japanese-style knife). All of these methods are acceptable ways to secure the handle. Beware of lower-quality knives with wood scales that appear to have true rivets but are actually simply glued to the tang.

ceramic knives

the new kid on the block

ALTHOUGH THEY'VE BEEN AROUND for twenty-five years, ceramic knives still feel like the Next Big Thing. Pull one out when you've got company, and it's almost guaranteed to turn heads just because it looks so different, almost like a toy (see page 5). It's no wonder ceramic gets people's attention: There hasn't been an innovation this dramatic in blade material for three thousand years.

What's the big appeal of ceramic? Mainly, it's sharp as can be and will stay that way for quite a while, thanks to its hardness (it's 50 percent harder than steel). Kyocera, which is the first and largest producer of ceramic blades, claims that the edge lasts ten times longer than an equivalent high-carbon stainless-steel blade. In addition to the classic white blade, they also have a more durable, higher-end line with a black blade, called Kyotop. The big downside to ceramic is its brittleness. A well-made ceramic knife won't shatter, but if you carelessly pull it out of the knife block, or just flat-out drop it, a piece of the tip or edge can chip off.

Other than its fragility, ceramic is impressive. It's light. It cuts so cleanly through soft foods like tomatoes that it feels like you're cutting through air. It's 100 percent nonreactive, so it will never stain, alter the flavor of food, or degrade with exposure to salts or acids. It's so smooth that almost nothing sticks to it—even starchy potato slices release fairly easily.

That said, ceramic knives aren't going to knock your steel blades off the chopping block just yet. They excel at everyday jobs like cutting vegetables, fruits, and boneless meat or fish, but to ram through the breastbone of a chicken or the hard rind of winter squash, you need the heft of a steel chef's knife. With virtually no flexibility, ceramic knives aren't meant for carving or boning a chicken. Ceramic makes a great addition to your collection, but it's not for everything.

With normal home use and proper care, a good-quality ceramic knife should stay relatively sharp for years, but the day will eventually come when you'll realize that it's no longer up to snuff. At that point, you can't simply pull out your favorite sharpening tool. Ceramic dulls differently than steel—the edge develops microscopic chips that require a special machine to remove. So you must pack the knife up and send it either to the original manufacturer (Kyocera offers free lifetime sharpening for all its blades, although you pay for shipping) or a designated ceramic sharpening service.

from powder to blade: the crafting of ceramic knives

Kyocera produces its knives in Sendai, a city in southwest Japan, from a natural material called zirconium dioxide, mined from mountains in Australia. The zirconium oxide is ground to a powder and then pulverized with water to make a very fine paste. This slurry is then pumped into a dryer that converts it back to a powder, which is then poured into a knife mold. The mold undergoes three hundred tons of pressure and comes out as a solid knife blank. From this point, the process follows a similar path as for steel blades, except instead of being tempered, ceramic blades are fired in a powerful furnace to harden them. Then a handle is attached, and the blades are polished, ground, honed, and buffed.

RAZOR SHARP AND FEATHER LIGHT, ceramic knives are perfect for dicing and slicing vegetables, fruits, and boneless meats. Just keep the following in mind in order to avoid damaging the blade.

DON'T carve, bone, or pry with ceramic, or use it for any purpose that requires twisting or flexing.

DON'T use it to cut frozen food or hard cheese.

know the limits of ceramic

DON'T use the side of the blade to smash garlic or other items, and never apply force to the side of the blade.

AVOID dropping or knocking the knife against a hard surface like a sink.

NEVER put the blade over an open flame.

knife-making capitals

GREAT KNIVES OF ALL TYPES are produced throughout the world, but a few regions in particular are known for their world-class kitchen cutlery.

germany

Germany is famous the world over for its high-quality forged knives. Everyone knows about Wüsthof and Zwilling JA Henckels, but there are many others producing well-made German knives, too.

The traditional German-style knife has a heavier, thicker blade with a big bolster. This style derives from German sword-making traditions of the Middle Ages. The region's medieval swords were, on the whole, large, weighty, and durable, the better to penetrate a knight's metal suit of armor. Brute force counted more than finesse, and swords were styled accordingly. As swordsmiths shifted over to forging kitchen cutlery, they retained the same approach.

For many people, German knives are practically synonymous with the name Solingen, which is often printed on the side of the blade. Solingen is the name of the city where virtually all German knives are made (it has dubbed itself the "city of blades"), but the name alone isn't necessarily a mark of quality.

japan

Not so long ago, few Western cooks paid much attention to Japanese knives. Now they're the talk of the town. Television chefs flaunt them, restaurant chefs covet them, home cooks are intrigued by them.

Japanese cooking knives have been around for more than a thousand years—the oldest-known chef's knife dates from earlier than A.D. 800. And just as in Germany, Japanese sword makers created the template for the modern Japanese knife. Whereas Ger-

man knights strove to bash in their enemy's metal plate of armor, samurai warriors hoped to behead their opponent. They needed precision swords—lightweight but also strong and very sharp—and master swordsmiths devised special techniques to accommodate them. When these craftsmen migrated from making swords to cutlery (a shift that largely occurred between 1800 and 1950), they applied their methods to knives.

There are two general types of Japanese knives. The traditional style has unique blade shapes and very specific functions (see page 41), and they're chisel ground to have a wide bevel on one side only. The best examples are forged by hand from a billet of steel, and they can be relatively thick and weighty. Contemporary-style Japanese knives emerged only in the last century. They resemble Western-style knives with a conventional double bevel and familiar shapes but the blades are thinner and lighter, and usually much sharper. This is the style that has so entranced the West in recent years.

Traditional Japanese carbon steel knives are mostly made in the city of Sakai, while stainless-steel knives are manufactured in the city of Seki. Both cities, like Solingen, have a centuries-long tradition of knife and sword making (Seki's moniker is "the city of swords"). Each stage of the knife-making process is handled by a different master craftsman. The finest knives pass through the hands of several artisans—one person forges the blade, another crafts the handle, another fits the handle to the blade—before completion.

france

The two biggest names in French cutlery are Sabatier and Laguiole.

Thirty or forty years ago, many people considered Sabatier (sah-BAH-tee-yay) knives to be among the best in the world, but the brand has since been diluted as a result of the countless low-quality knock-offs now on the market. The original carbon steel Sabatier knives were manufactured by two families in the town of Thiers beginning in the early 1800s (see page 5 for photo). Eventually, other cutlers in town borrowed the name for their own blades. Today, several knife manufacturers in Thiers continue to make high-quality forged Sabatier-branded knives, in both carbon steel and stainless steel. To distinguish themselves from one another, each company applies a unique logo to the blade; one manufacturer that's popular with U.S. retailers is Thiers-Issard, which uses four stars and an elephant. Although these French manufacturers have formed an association to try to protect the Sabatier brand, the name is unregulated around the world and appears on knives made in China and elsewhere.

The name Laguiole (lay-ohl) refers both to a town in southern France and a style of knife. It is not a brand. The original type was a pocket knife, sometimes with an attached corkscrew. The first folding knife made in Laguiole dates back to 1829; it was reportedly inspired by the Spanish pocket knife, called a *navaja,* which Laguiole shepherds encountered after spending a winter in Catalonia. Nowadays, the Laguiole name is also associated with steak knives, wine openers, and other kitchen accessories. Made by a number of different French manufacturers, most of them based in Thiers (rather than Laguiole), hand-crafted Laguiole knives feature a bee emblem (there's a long-running argument over whether it's actually a fly), and the handles may be elaborately designed and made of bone or another unusual material (see red-handled knives on page 38). Unfortunately, since the name isn't licensed, Laguiole knives have suffered a similar fate as Sabatier knives, with many cheaply made non-French versions on the market.

To be certain you're getting a genuine Sabatier or Laguiole knife, ask the vendor for the name, and perhaps the contact information, of the producer in France. A reputable retailer should be willing to provide it.

italy

Italy has a few large manufacturers, particularly in the sporting-knife category, but high-quality kitchen cutlery is something of a cottage industry. The countryside is dotted with artisans producing knives on a very small scale, often dedicating themselves to a single type of knife. To compete in an intense marketplace, these cutlers have united into consortiums to distribute the knives to international buyers. Keep your eyes peeled, and you may come across a pair of beautiful poultry shears crafted by an artisan in Maniago, or one-of-a-kind knives from a maker in Scarperia, a tiny town near Florence (see page 42).

england

The city of Sheffield was once a leading producer of kitchen cutlery and, although some knives are still made there, the industry is now a shell of its former self. But Sheffield's place in history is secure. It's the birthplace of stainless steel and the original Granton edge (see page 33). Just as with Solingen, some knives bear the name Sheffield on the blade, but this doesn't guarantee a great knife.

united states

The United States has many small cutlery companies, and countless more craftsmen producing boutique knives out of their garages, but there isn't a particular city or region known for its cooking knives the way Solingen and Seki are. Most U.S. knifemakers follow the German style with its big bolsters and thicker, heavier blades. Dexter Russell and LamsonSharp are two large manufacturers, both based in Massachusetts.

Making knives connects me to our past (as "man, the toolmaker"), and to people today who want to slow down and create good food with a beautiful and highly functional tool.

—Bob Kramer, master bladesmith, Olympia, Washington

MOST OF US HAVE A FAVORITE KNIFE that we use all the time, mainly because it's comfortable and gets the job done. There's nothing wrong with that—plenty of top chefs do the same thing. The fact is, nearly all your everyday cutting can be done with just a couple of knives: your chef's knife and paring knife. However, it's also true that some knives have special talents, and if you know what they are, you can call on them at the right moment. Boning knives, cheese knives, slicers, carvers . . . maybe you already have these knives in your drawer but don't know when to use them, or perhaps you've seen them in shops and wondered if you really need them. Now's your chance to find out.

a blade for every purpose

FROM LEFT, FIVE DIFFERENT
TIPS: pronged, sheep's foot,
rounded, spear point,
trailing point

I probably have $30,000 worth of knives. My most expensive was
about $1,800. It's a beautiful Alaskan hand-crafted salmon knife.
I've used it probably four times, but I fell in love with the handle.

—Rick Tramonto, author, restaurateur, and chef at Tru

how to decode a knife's function

THERE'S A REASON why boning knives have that swooped-up tip and vegetable cleavers have a straight edge. The shape of a blade can clue you in to its purpose, and when you factor in its thickness and flexibility, you'll have a pretty good picture of what a knife can do.

the tip

Notice the many types of points. Each one has a particular function.

PRONGED: Used to spear food, such as a cube of cheese or slice of tomato.

SHEEP'S FOOT, OR SNUB-NOSED: Creates a straight edge right to the tip, but still offers a sharp point for piercing, puncturing, or scoring.

ROUNDED, OR BLUNT: Indicates that the knife isn't meant to pierce or puncture food. Can also be a safety feature.

SPEAR POINT: A versatile tip that's good for piercing, puncturing, scoring, and more (such as testing vegetables for doneness, coring fruit, flicking out lemon seeds, stemming greens, opening packages). The shape forces the cutting edge to curve up toward the tip, which allows the blade to rock.

TRAILING POINT: Seen on boning and fillet knives. Separates meat from bone without piercing the flesh.

blade thickness

All blades are thin along the cutting edge. But look to the thickness of the spine (see photo on page 48) to give you an idea of how tough and how sharp the knife might be. A thick spine makes for a heavier and tougher knife, good for cracking through bones, shells, or very dense vegetables such as butternut squash. A very thin blade makes a lighter, sharper, more flexible knife, which lets you cut thin slices of meat or vegetables. A good guideline: the thinner the knife, the thinner the slice.

blade length

The length of the blade tells you how much you can do with a single stroke. Long blades cut cleanly through meat or fish and can make quick work of a big pile of spinach. Shorter blades are easier to maneuver when you're peeling something, such as an apple in your hand, and they let you cut smaller items on the board more precisely.

blade flexibility

If you encounter a blade that's flexible, it could be meant to fillet fish or bone meat (the flexibility makes it easier to navigate around bones), or it might be intended to carve a roast or slice a salmon. But flexibility can also be a sign of a cheaply made knife.

blade width

A wide blade suggests that the knife is meant for on-the-board chopping (the width provides knuckle clearance), whereas knives with narrow blades are often meant to be used in other ways.

edge curvature

The curve of the edge can sometimes tell you what cutting motion works best. A blade with a slight belly makes it easier to use a rocking motion while chopping. A straight edge is good for straight down or forward slicing.

edge type

The cutting edge is either straight or serrated. The edge type can hint at the type of food and the stroke to use. Serrated edges perform best with a sawing motion, and they're often intended for foods with hard crusts and soft or delicate interiors.

I like a clunky heavy European style knife, like a Wüsthof. I have big hands. It's uncomfortable for me to work with a really narrow blade.
—David Waltuck, chef-owner of Chanterelle

FROM LEFT: Sabatier 8-inch, Henckels Twin Four Star II 8-inch, Wüsthof Classic Ikon 8-inch, Henckels Professional "S" 10-inch, Wüsthof Classic 8-inch (with crow's beak handle)

chef's knives

EVERY TIME YOU COOK, you're going to use your chef's knife. It's for chopping, slicing, dicing, and mincing just about any ingredient you come across. It's the ultimate all-purpose knife: wide enough to give you plenty of knuckle clearance when you're working on a cutting board; long enough to cut large items efficiently and small items precisely; and curved enough to let you rock the blade as you chop.

Chef's knives, sometimes called cook's knives, range from 4 to 14 inches in length. For your first one, you can't go wrong with an 8-incher. But don't be afraid to try out a longer 10-inch knife, which can cut efficiently through things like watermelons and big piles of fresh herbs and greens. If you're intimidated by large knives, a 6-inch chef's knife can be perfect. And don't overlook the adorable 4-inch size—it's easy to maneuver and fun to use, just right for chopping a few capers or cutting a basil chiffonade.

Chef's knives fall into two general types: European-style and Japanese-style blades.

european style

European-style blades are on the thicker and heavier side, and they traditionally have a big bolster, which is the portion of metal that extends from the handle down to the heel of the blade. The bolster can act as a finger guard, allowing you to choke up on the blade more securely. It also adds weight to the knife, and it makes the heel thicker and stronger, which is ideal for hacking through bone or halving a winter squash. However, a full bolster can become an impediment when sharpening; over time, the edge can develop a notch right at the spot where the heel thickens. To address this issue, some European knifemakers are now producing knives with a half-bolster (see third from left in photo opposite) or no bolster, more akin to a Japanese-style knife. European knives also tend to be fairly thick along the spine—the blade tapers gradually from spine to cutting edge—which supplies additional heft and strength to the knife.

Within this category, there are German- and French-style blades. The German style has a pronounced curve to the edge and a wider blade, and the French style is leaner and straighter. The difference can be subtle, but some people do have a preference.

Once I was introduced to the world of Japanese knives, I began to understand the value of a sharp, light knife. You can do more work with them and your hand doesn't get tired. You instantly become a better cook.
—Vitaly Paley, chef-owner of Paley's Place

FROM LEFT: Shun Elite 8-inch, Shun Classic 8-inch, Global 8-inch chef's knife, Shun Elite 10-inch, Shun Classic 6-inch, Shun Elite 4-inch

japanese style

Sometimes called a *gyuto*, the Japanese-style chef's knife is very similar to a European chef's knife; the main differences are the bolster, the blade thickness, and the weight. The bolster, if the knife has one, is just a collar of metal near the handle; there's no wedge of steel descending to the heel of the blade. The absence of a bolster can feel a little precarious if you're used to pinching the blade between your thumb and forefinger, so you might want to use a different grip with these knives, keeping your fingers farther back on the handle.

Japanese-style chef's knives are thinner than their European counterparts, and this makes for a sharper knife: There's simply less mass to push through food. There's a trade-off, though; the finer edge tends to need more frequent maintenance and sharpening to keep in top form. Also, since they're not as beefy as German-style knives, these blades can't bulldoze their way through tough cutting jobs as easily, and doing so risks dulling the edge. This style of knife tends to be more lightweight, and some cooks find that appealing. Lighter knives can be easier to control and less fatiguing during a long chopping session.

Professional Japanese chefs use many different kinds of knives, each one specific to the food they're cutting. But Japanese homemakers want one knife to do everything—to cut fish, vegetables, and meat—and that's the purpose of the santoku. It's easy to handle and it's not too big; it's perfect for the home cook.

—Hideji Asanuma, chef de cuisine at 15 East

FROM TOP: Füri Rachael Ray Gusto-Grip East/West 5-inch, Wüsthof Classic hollow-edge 5-inch, Kikuichi Elite Warikomi Damascus Tsuchime all-purpose 8-inch

santoku knives

THE SANTOKU LOOKS LIKE a small chef's knife with a rounded tip. It originated in Japan, where it is the homemaker's all-purpose knife, but the santoku has become hugely popular in the United States and is now outselling European chef's knives. The name translates roughly as "three uses" (or three benefits, virtues, or values)—it's for slicing fish, cutting meat, and chopping vegetables—in contrast to traditional Japanese shapes, which have more specific functions.

The classic santoku shape features a relatively straight cutting edge, which works well with a forward and backward stroke or straight-down chop, both typical Japanese ways of cutting. The santoku revolution in the United States has led to versions with more curvature, which are easier to rock-chop. The rounded nose of a santoku can score but not pierce food, and its shorter blade (between five and eight inches) means it's not very efficient on large volumes, although if you're a novice cook, its compactness can be reassuring. A santoku is a cool knife, no doubt, and a nice addition to your knife set, but it's not as versatile as the classic chef's knife and probably not a replacement for it.

By the way, don't confuse the divots often seen on the side of the blade with the santoku shape. They're an add-on feature, and they don't necessarily improve the knife's performance (see "The Story of the Granton Edge," page 33).

You say santoku, I say santuko: You'll hear it both ways, but for the record, the Japanese pronunciation is sahn-toh-koo.

We do kind of old-fashioned things here. We do vegetables tournéed.
Some people feel they need that special curved knife to do their tournées.
Other people do perfect tournées with a butter knife.
—David Waltuck, chef-owner of Chanterelle

TOP, FROM LEFT: Classic spear point parer,
sheep's foot parer, tournet knife
BOTTOM, FROM TOP: granny knife, serrated parer,
fluting knife

paring knives

WITH A BLADE between 2 and 4½ inches long, a paring knife does all the things that a chef's knife cannot do. It peels fruits and vegetables, hulls strawberries, cores tomatoes, deveins shrimp, scores peaches, segments oranges, trims pie dough, and much more. It can navigate tight spots—helpful when boning a chicken thigh—and you can choke up on it to get more control of the tip, as you might for removing potato eyes. Whenever you need to make small, fine cuts, a paring knife is a good choice. Paring knives come in a variety of shapes.

classic spear point parer

The most versatile of all parers, this is sometimes used as a mini-chef's knife to slice or dice small ingredients like shallots or garlic cloves, but it's most practical for in-the-hand cutting, or for any task that requires just a little extra control or precision. A good all-purpose blade length is 3 or 3½ inches.

sheep's-foot parer

The blunted tip makes this parer somewhat safer for peeling vegetables; however, it can't remove potato eyes or core tomatoes. Sometimes called a European parer, it can slice small ingredients on a cutting board, although its straighter edge means it won't rock that well.

tournet knife

Also called a bird's beak knife or turning knife, the original purpose of this petite parer was to carve potatoes into mini footballs, which is still done in classic French restaurants. The curved edge removes more of the skin in one swipe, and in the fast pace of a restaurant, that's key. Although you probably don't *tourner* many potatoes, you could use a *tournet* knife to peel any round fruit or vegetable. It's virtually useless for on-the-board cutting.

granny knife

This is what an old-fashioned carbon steel paring knife looks like after years and years of sharpening (see photo opposite). The shape may not be ideal, but it brings up warm memories for some folks, so a handful of manufacturers make them as a novelty item. It's good for peeling and trimming, but not so great for on-the-board chopping.

serrated parer

This new parer makes a nice little bar knife for lemons and limes: The serrated edge bites into the rind easily and stays sharper for longer. You could also use it to halve cherry tomatoes.

fluting knife

The triangular blade on this knife is meant for decorating or garnishing fruits and vegetables. It's perfect for fluting mushroom caps or making tomato rosettes and it can substitute for a classic parer, but it's not an essential.

FROM LEFT: L'Economie 8-inch, Global 8¾-inch, Wüsthof super slicer, Shun Elite 9-inch

bread knives

A SERRATED BREAD KNIFE is indispensable for slicing everything from New York bagels to Parisian baguettes, and it can also pinch-hit when your straight-edge knives are a little dull; it excels at slicing tomatoes and lemons, peeling pineapples or melons, slicing cured sausage or a crispy breaded chicken breast, or cutting anything that's harder outside than it is inside. The serrated edge bites cleanly into firm rinds and crusts without crushing what lies beneath.

The type of serrations on bread knives varies quite a bit, and it's impossible to predict the performance of one style or another just by looking at it. As a general rule, though, bread knives with very pointed teeth and recessed scallops are better at penetrating crusty artisanal breads, but they tend to rip through softer interiors. Wavy serrations are gentler on tender loaves, giving cleaner slices with fewer crumbs; they're better for slicing things like focaccia, Italian bread, or tender pastries, or for cutting a cake into layers.

Regardless of the serrations, the ideal bread knife has a long, rigid blade and an offset handle. The typical 8-inch blade is fine for slicing a baguette or sandwich bread, but it comes up just a little too short for larger *boules*. A 9- or 10-inch knife is a better choice. Rigidity is important, because a blade that flexes can slip and can lead to uneven slices, especially on denser loaves. And an offset handle lets you slice right through to the bottom crust without bumping your knuckles; unfortunately, most bread knives don't have this useful feature.

You don't need to spend a fortune on a bread knife, but keep in mind that some of the least expensive ones are too flexible or have ineffective serrations. Try to do a test drive before buying.

If I had to choose one knife, it would be a utility knife with a six-to eight-inch blade. I can slice, bone, and chop with it. It's relatively narrow so there's not as much clearance for your fingers, but it's enough.

—Jacques Pépin, chef, cooking show host, teacher, and author

FROM LEFT: Berti carver, Wüsthof Classic 10-inch ham slicer, Wüsthof Classic 7-inch fillet knife, Wüsthof Classic 12-inch salmon slicer, Shun 6-inch utility knife, Viking 8-inch carving knife

slicers and carvers

THESE KNIVES GO BY MANY DIFFERENT NAMES; one brand's carving knife is another brand's slicer. Don't try to figure out the naming conventions. Just look for the one with the length and flexibility you need. There are basically two types of slicers, those with pointed tips and those with rounded tips.

pointed-tip carvers

Lighter, longer, and narrower than a chef's knife, these knives, which may be called carvers or slicers, are meant for slicing roast turkey, London broil, pork loin, leg of lamb, or any other large hunk of roasted or grilled meat or poultry. The pointed tip is useful for cutting into joints or working around a bone, and the long blade averts shearing the flesh with excessive sawing. Blade lengths range from 8 to 14 inches, with 9 inches being a good all-purpose size, but the general rule is that the blade should be an inch or two longer than the food you're slicing. Shorter versions (sometimes called sandwich knives or utility knives) are useful if you work in a deli or make a lot of turkey clubs at home, but otherwise they won't see much use. Slicers with serrated edges exist, but they're not ideal for cutting through meat.

rounded-tip slicers

This category subdivides into two knife types: ham slicers and salmon slicers. Ham slicers are fairly rigid and wide, and they often feature a divoted Granton edge (see page 33) to reduce sticking and help the knife move cleanly through the meat; an ideal length is 10 inches. Salmon slicers are exceptionally thin, long, and flexible, the better to yield translucent slices of cured Nova lox (remember: the thinner the knife, the thinner the slice). Its foot-long blade allows full, smooth strokes that won't tear up delicate fish.

Both ham and salmon slicers have rounded tips to prevent you from accidentally piercing the flesh when the blade changes direction.

> I love my Nenox knives. That's what I gravitate toward. If I'm doing certain filleting or vegetable knife work, I'll go to my Massimo knives, the ones with the dimples in them. I'm knife specific. I just don't grab a knife to grab a knife.
> —Rick Tramonto, author, restaurateur, and chef at Tru

utility knife

It's a fixture in many knife sets, but for many cooks, the utility knife (which ranges between 4½ to 8 inches in length) is in a sort of no-man's land. The problem is that it's too short for slicing meat, too long for trimming vegetables in hand, too narrow for chopping on the board (no knuckle clearance). But every knife seems to have its fans, and the utility knife is no exception. Novice cooks may prefer it to a big chef's knife, and some pros with large hands use it as an oversized paring knife.

boning knives

The boning knife's most distinctive feature is its tapered tip—called a trailing point—which helps you separate meat from bone without puncturing the flesh unnecessarily. It's meant to be used with short, backward swipes of the knife. If you find yourself frequently boning a whole chicken or leg of lamb, trimming silver-skin, or butterflying boneless meats, this thin, narrow knife will come in handy. But it's one of those knives with fairly limited use for most home cooks. You'll see both flexible and stiff boning knives—a moderate amount of flex is helpful for boning a chicken breast, whereas a stiffer blade is better for Frenching a rack of lamb—but it's personal preference which type you like. They range from 5 to 8 inches, and 6 inches is a nice, versatile size. More important than size and flexibility is the edge itself: keep it sharp. Smaller boning knives, called trimming knives, allow for more precision when working on smaller birds.

fillet knives

The wickedly thin, narrow, and sharp blade on this knife is exactly what's needed to efficiently skin or fillet a whole fish. It's incredibly flexible, the better to follow the contours of the bones and leave no waste. You probably don't need a fillet knife—that's what fishmongers are for. But if you're an avid angler, or if you think you'll enjoy the process of learning how to skin your own salmon fillets, you'll appreciate a good fillet knife. It can also double as a knife for cutting medium-firm cheeses.

THE DIVOTED EDGE that's become almost synonymous with santoku knives was born in 1928, when the Granton knife company in Sheffield, England, ground divots into its long slicing knives. The series of oval divots, which alternate on each side of the blade, thinned the cutting edge while maintaining rigidity. This novel design permitted thinner slices, and the air pockets created by the divots seemed to reduce friction and sticking. When Granton's patent expired, other knifemakers began applying the divots on their slicers.

the story of the granton edge

That might have been the end of the story if Wüsthof hadn't ground divots onto its santokus in the 1990s. Since then, the dimpled look has become something of a fashion statement, and they're now slapped onto the side of parers, chef's knives, utility knives, you name it. And the edge might be called fluted, scalloped, dimpled, hollow edge, or *kullenschliff*. When you see the divots, take a careful look. They can only do their thing if they come right down to the cutting edge—if they run along the middle of the blade, they're probably doing more for the look of the knife than anything else.

I'm dependent on my Chinese cleaver for everything from slicing and dicing vegetables to chopping fine herbs, mincing things very small, smashing garlic, and flattening chicken breast.

—Joyce Goldstein, author and former chef-owner of Square One restaurant

FROM TOP: Shun 7¾-inch Chinese chef's knife/vegetable cleaver, Global 6-inch meat cleaver, Wüsthof 6-inch forged meat cleaver

cleavers

CLEAVERS COME IN TWO VARIETIES—those for meat and those for vegetables—and it's not hard to tell them apart. Both have large, broad blades, but a meat cleaver is solid and weighty, like a Mack truck, whereas a vegetable cleaver is light and zippy, like a sports car.

meat cleaver

You can recognize a meat cleaver by its thick blade, which barely tapers from the spine down to the edge. The edge itself is beveled at a very wide angle, almost like a wedge, so it's durable even if not remarkably sharp. Weighing in at anywhere from two to five pounds, meat cleavers deliver crushing force on the downward stroke, perfect for chopping through bones. If you need to halve chicken thighs for cracklings or split a chicken breast, a meat cleaver is your best choice (although to be sure, a good butcher with a bandsaw will do the job more cleanly, without splintering the bone). You can use the side or spine of the blade to pound veal into scaloppine or beef into carpaccio, and you can use the heel as a pick, to chip apart a block of frozen shrimp, for example, a job that would outright destroy any other knife. Too large for knife blocks or drawer inserts, meat cleavers often feature a hole in the blade for hanging on a hook.

vegetable cleaver

The Chinese version of the European chef's knife, this cleaver looks like a giant razor blade, and in a sense, it acts like one too, splitting vegetables quickly with a simple downward stroke. Its blade is thin and light, and once you're used to it, it slices, dices, minces, and juliennes as efficiently as your chef's knife (skilled users can even make it rock-chop). The wide blade supports the food being cut and can act as a scoop to ferry vegetables from the board to the pan.

"Trying to get a knife sharp enough to cut a tomato is overrated. Just use a serrated knife."

—Tom Douglas, chef, restaurateur, radio show host, and author

FROM LEFT: set of Shun Elite steak knifes,
Wüsthof Classic 5-inch tomato knife

tomato and steak knives

tomato knives

If your chef's knife was always finely honed, there'd be no reason to own a tomato knife. But that's a big "if," and since a serrated edge slices tomatoes better than a not-so-sharp straight edge, the tomato knife does meet a need. It's shorter and thinner than a bread knife, with smaller serrations, so it's just a little better suited to the size and shape of a tomato. Some versions have a pronged tip, meant for lifting the slice onto a sandwich or plate.

steak knives

We don't use a serrated knife to slice prime rib or carve leg of lamb, so why should we use one at the dinner table? Well, we shouldn't. A very sharp straight-edged knife is so much more civilized, severing meat fibers cleanly and smoothly. To get a sense of the experience, try using a sharp paring knife the next time you tuck into a grilled porterhouse. A straight-edged steak knife needs frequent maintenance—scraping the knife against a ceramic dinner plate is about the worst thing you can do to the edge—but sharpening it is quick with the right tool. For those in the know, straight-edged steak knives are definitely a thing, albeit an expensive thing. (They start at about $25 apiece, and $300 for a set of four isn't that unusual.)

I bought my favorite knife at Dehillerin, the be-all and end-all cook's-equipment store in Paris. I also bought smaller versions to use as steak knives in the restaurant. We sharpen them ourselves with little handheld gadgets. The waiters can do it. I just wish they would do it more often.
—Steve Johnson, chef-owner of Rendezvous

cheese knives

IT'S ALWAYS A LITTLE DISTURBING when you set out a lovely wedge of, say, Spanish manchego at a party and then watch as it gets hacked into a misshapen mess. Often the culprits are the guests—most people just don't pay attention when they slice cheese—but sometimes the problem is the knife. For the cleanest cuts, you've got to match the utensil to the texture of the cheese.

1. spreadable cheese

For gooey cheeses like Taleggio, soft Gorgonzola, ripe Epoisses, and Spanish torta del Casar, you don't need a knife so much as a flat, broad spatula that will smear the cheese onto a cracker. It's worth having a spreading knife or two on hand—they're inexpensive, and their ornamental handles (often kitschy, but there's sure to be one you'll like) will liven up a cheese board. If you don't have a spreader, just use a butter knife.

2. soft cheese

Soft cheeses like fresh chèvre and not-too-ripe Brie won't slice cleanly with a knife; they just get smushy. So the best tool for these moist varieties is a cheese wire—not the type with a roller behind the wire, or the type where the wire is hinged to the cheese board. You need something simple: the kind with a metal rod that's been bent into a U is perfect.

3. semisoft to semifirm cheese

This broad category includes all the different types of Cheddars, along with Havarti, Monterey jack, Jarlsberg, Gouda, and so many more. These moderately moist cheeses tend to stick to knives. To avoid this, you want to minimize the surface area of the blade; choose a cheese knife with a very thin, narrow blade or a skeleton knife with large holes punched out of the blade (and ideally a straight edge rather than serrated edge). In a pinch, you could use a filleting or boning knife to slice these softer-style cheeses.

4. firm cheese

For drier, denser varieties like manchego, Cantal, or Gruyère, you'll want a larger, heftier knife that gives you extra leverage and control. When you're cutting slices or cubes in the kitchen, a long chef's knife does the job nicely. Set one hand on the tip of the knife to help push it through. If you're putting the cheese out for guests, set out a mini-cleaver-shaped cheese knife, or any knife with a wider, sturdy blade.

5. hard, crumbly cheese

For hard cheeses like Parmigiano-Reggiano and pecorino, you're often aiming for chunks that you can grate. For that you need a rigid teardrop or flat-edged blade that you can pry into the wedge. If you lack a Parmesan knife, use the thicker heel (not the fragile tip) of a European-style chef's knife.

FROM LEFT: All Kikuichi knives: usuba kasumi 7-inch slicing knife, yanagi kasumi blue Damascus 12-inch sushi knife, takohiki kasumi white sushi knife, honesuki 7-inch slicing knife, deba kasumitogi 6-inch chef's knife

traditional japanese knives

PERHAPS MORE THAN ANY OTHER CULTURE, the Japanese are religious about their knives and how they're used. In their cuisine, texture is almost considered an ingredient itself, and presentation is elevated to an art. From slicing sushi to carving carrot spirals, the goal is clean, precise cuts. To get there, they need just the right knife, honed to an exquisitely sharp edge.

Traditional Japanese knives are chisel ground, meaning they're beveled on one side of the blade only (for right-handers, the bevel is on the right side). Also, the entire back side of the blade is usually slightly concave, which releases surface tension on very moist food to minimize sticking. The bevel is often quite high, rising ½ inch or more up the side of the blade, which directs food away from the blade during slicing. The high bevel also makes the knife much easier to sharpen manually on a stone, something Japanese chefs will do several times a day. The trickiest part of stone sharpening is maintaining a consistent angle, and the high bevel on these knives serves as a built-in angle guide. Single-bevel knives are intended for either left- or right-handed users, so if you're left-handed, you'll need to special order a model with the bevel on the left side of the blade.

These knives are task specific: each shape has a unique function, such as slicing fish or boning meat or cutting vegetables. Many manufacturers now make contemporary versions, retaining the traditional shape but applying a modern double bevel to the edge.

usuba

Like a narrower version of the Chinese cleaver, this is typically used for slicing vegetables. Japanese chefs use the usuba for on-the-board chopping or in their hand, as Western chefs use a paring knife. The nakiri is the contemporary style, with a double-beveled edge.

yanagi and takohiki

The long, narrow yanagi is used for making straight and diagonal cuts of fish for sushi and sashimi. The blades range from 8 to 13 inches long. The length allows the cook to slice through the fish cleanly with a single backward stroke, so there is as little disturbance to the flesh as possible. The takohiki (sometimes called a takobiki) is a variation on the yanagi. The blunted tip is preferred for preparing octopus (tako).

honesuki

Primarily used for boning poultry, the angled tip on this blade eases its way around joints and bones. The blade length is usually 5 or 6 inches.

deba

The thick, heavy deba (DEH-ba) is traditionally meant for filleting fish or for cutting up boneless meat, but it works rather nicely for cutting up a whole chicken, too, since it's hefty enough to crack through bones yet narrow enough to nose into tight areas. Modern double-beveled versions of the deba are light and thin, essentially making it into a small chef's knife.

shears

kitchen shears

Every cook needs a good pair of kitchen shears. They're handy for cutting parchment paper or kitchen twine, clipping the tops off bags, and lots more—they're like scissors on steroids. And they often cut faster and cleaner than a knife, especially if your cutting skills aren't quite up to par. Reach for shears next time you have to snip chives, trim pie dough, chop canned tomatoes, cut raw bacon, slice dried fruit, trim fat from raw poultry, portion pizza, or cut food into kid-size pieces.

Kitchen shears typically have fairly wide handles and short, durable blades, for more power when cutting. Some are designed only for right-handed users, but most are ambidextrous. Good-quality shears have stainless-steel blades that are held together at the fulcrum by a screw or, even better, a come-apart joint that permits the blades to be separated for easier cleaning. A riveted fulcrum is usually a sign of lower quality, and it makes cleaning and sharpening more difficult.

Before buying, try the shears on for size if possible. The handles should fit snugly and have rounded edges for comfort. Many shears have extra features, such as a bottle or jar opener, that sound great but in reality don't often get much use. Kitchen shears with spring-loaded designs aren't especially helpful, and they can be fussy: They must be clipped closed, they trap bits of food, and they're more work to clean.

poultry shears

Poultry shears were designed for one main task: to power through the bones and cartilage of a roasted chicken or other small bird. They're not the best tool for cutting up a raw chicken, however; for that task, you'll have an easier time and get more refined results with a chef's knife. Poultry shears do have other uses, though. They're handy for clawing through lobster and crab shells, trimming large flower stems, or any other rough job that would beat up your kitchen shears or chef's knife. Spring-loaded for extra leverage, the classic poultry shear has thick, strong curved blades. Some models have a helpful notch toward the back of the blade to grab onto the bone. When shopping, look for an overall heaviness, with stainless-steel blades that feel solid and sharp.

tip **WHATEVER YOU DO, don't drop your shears. This knocks the blades out of alignment, and as the off-kilter blades scrape against each other, they quickly go dull.**

BUYING KNIVES CAN BE DAUNTING. First, there's the mind-numbing variety: You have to choose among dozens of brands and styles, knives from different countries, knives with different materials. And there's the expense: A few good-quality knives will set you back two or three hundred dollars, and perhaps quite a bit more. And finally there's the commitment: These guys will be your daily companions in the kitchen for many years, if not for life. It's a big investment, and you want to do it right. And you will, as long as you remember that buying a knife is a personal matter, like choosing your friends. There's no best knife for everyone; there's only a best knife for you. The tips that follow will help you find your way.

on becoming a savvy knife shopper

have a plan

Before you start, ask yourself a few questions. How many and what types of knives do you need? Are you committed to a matching set or will you choose each knife individually? What's your price range? If you're going for lifetime quality, you'll need to spend more. But if you don't intend to treat your knives like royalty, you might want to shop at the lower end of the scale. Consider whether to buy a sharpener and a storage system at the same time. You probably should; you'll need them to keep your knives at their best. If you've thought about these things in advance, you'll be less likely to become confused when you're staring at rows and rows of gorgeous knives at the store.

tip A BETTER WEDDING GIFT: Instead of buying a set of knives for the newlyweds, consider giving a gift certificate to a well-stocked cookware shop (along with this book) so they can hand-pick their favorites.

where to buy

Use the Internet to do preliminary research if you'd like, but when the time comes to actually buy, your laptop won't suffice. You need to get out there and get your hands on the knives. Head to a dedicated cutlery store or serious cookware shop, or any place that offers a wide selection of high-quality products and a knowledgeable sales staff. Good retailers will not only inform you about their products but will also try to help find the knife that best fits your hand. You should feel encouraged to try out as many as necessary, and you shouldn't feel pushed toward one knife or another.

Even better than holding the knife is getting to cut with it—not so much to judge sharpness but simply to know how it feels in action. Call the store in advance to see if this is permitted, and if so, bring along a few apples, carrots, and tomatoes. If you're shopping for a good bread knife, you might show up with a favorite crusty loaf (with bread knives, you'll want to pay attention to performance as well as comfort, because serrated edges vary in effectiveness).

> Someone might tell you that an $800 knife is full of hooey, but actually, it's not. I gave one to my husband—we own about two hundred knives—and that's probably the only one he uses. It sits out in a wood shield.
>
> —Nancy Oakes, chef-owner of Boulevard restaurant, author of *Boulevard, The Cookbook*

how to evaluate a knife

BUYING A KNIFE is a little like buying shoes: You have to try it out to know how it fits. If it's all wrong, you'll know right away. If it feels okay, take a few minutes to give it a test drive. Do some mock chopping (or real chopping, if allowed). Try to imagine how you'll feel after a big meal's worth of slicing and dicing. Check out each part of the knife, as described below. Above all, trust yourself: If you don't like something—how the knife feels in your hand or how it rocks on the board—it doesn't matter how sleek it looks, or how much someone else is raving about it. When you pick up a knife and it feels utterly natural, almost like it's always been there, you know you've found the one for you.

knife anatomy

Here are some tips on assessing the different parts and characteristics of a knife.

1. handle

There are many different styles of handles, ranging from nouveau designs and materials to the more traditional. Aesthetics aside, there are some functional differences among them. Rubber or plastic handles come in molded and ergonomic forms, they're hygienic, and they can be textured in order to feel more "grippy." You may or may not like that. Metal handles feel solid and professional to some, but cold and slippery to others. Wood handles are pleasing, but they can require more maintenance (prolonged exposure to water will damage them). Traditional Japanese wooden handles are made of a soft unvarnished wood that's simply planed into a cylindrical shape. With use, these handles conform to your hand for a customized fit.

Regardless of the material, the handle should feel comfortable and secure. Some contoured handles feel good in one position but awkward in another, so vary your grip. With a paring knife, hold the knife as you would for peeling an apple as well as for cutting on a board. With a chef's knife, notice if your hand wants to slip forward as you chop, or if you're inclined to squeeze too hard to get a better grip. Do you have enough knuckle clearance? How will the handle feel when it's wet? Do you prefer a handle whose end curls down at the back (called a crow's beak, see page 20), or do you like a flat butt, as is typical on Japanese-style knives? Once you focus on the differences, you may find you have an instinctive preference.

2. heel

Check the corner of the heel; on some knives it's acutely sharp and on others it's rounded off just enough to avoid the accidental nick.

3. bolster

This is the portion of metal that connects the blade to the handle. On traditional European-style knives, the bolster extends right down to the heel. Besides adding a lot of weight, this creates a sort of cushion, or guard, for your fingers, depending on your grip. If you're uneasy holding a large chef's knife, a big bolster can feel safer. On the other hand, a bolster that extends to the heel makes sharpening more difficult, because the heel won't fit through the slots on manual and electric sharpeners. With time, the heel can develop a notch where sharpening

Cutting edge

Spine

Heel

Bolster

Tang

Handle

stops. A professional can repair the damage, but if you want to avoid the problem in the first place, you may want a knife with a half-bolster. On Japanese-style knives (see page 22), the bolster is simply a metal collar between the handle and blade, and there's no cushion to protect your fingers.

4. spine

Notice how thick and how smooth this top ridge of the knife is. If the spine is harsh and sharply squared off, as opposed to polished and soft, the edges can dig into your skin.

5. the tang

The tang is the strip of metal that protrudes from the blade, and it has two main functions: it provides a surface to attach the handle, and it helps balance the knife. Tangs come in a variety of lengths and shapes—a full tang continues to the end of the handle, and a partial tang stops somewhere in the middle—but it's not fair to make blanket statements about which is better. Some European knives may need a full tang to counter their heavy blades, but lighter Japanese knives may benefit from a stubbier tang. It all depends on the particular knife. Instead of focusing on the tang, which may not even be visible, look instead to the balance and weight of the knife.

6. the cutting edge

It's tempting to judge a knife by how sharp it is, but that's actually not the most important quality when selecting a knife. Store display knives are rarely at their peak sharpness and, unlike the knife's weight, handle, and bolster, which won't change, the edge is dynamic. That said, if the knife feels seriously dull, you might ask to try a brand-new specimen, just to get a sense of its potential. The salesperson should be able to tell you which knives are better able to hold a keen edge and which are easier to sharpen (it depends greatly on the type of steel). Also notice the edge curvature and whether it's appropriate for your cutting style. For instance, a knife with a straight edge won't rock-chop as smoothly as one with more of a belly.

blade material

You can't assess the quality of the steel by sight, but a knowledgeable salesperson should be able to explain the characteristics of the steel alloys used by various brands. You might probe the matter with a few questions: How easily does this knife take an edge? How durable is the edge? How resistant to corrosion is the knife? (No steel is completely rustproof.) Is the blade fairly tough, or is it more on the brittle side? No knife will score perfectly in all areas, so it's up to you to decide which traits you care about most. If you're shopping for a ceramic knife, ask about warranty and replacement information in case the knife chips.

Get a knife that's balanced and weighted for you. There's no reason you shouldn't get fitted for a knife the way you get fitted for anything else, like a dress, a suit, or a pair of skis.
—Tom Douglas, chef, restaurateur, radio show host, and author

weight

The weight of a knife, particularly a chef's knife, can make you either love it or hate it. Cooks who prefer weighty knives say the heft helps them cut ("the knife does the work for you"), but you do work harder on the up slice. Others find a lightweight knife easier to maneuver; it makes them feel agile and in control, and they cut more precisely as a result. But if a lightweight knife feels like it's going to fly out of your hand, it's not for you. The only way to discover which camp you're in is to try out a bunch of knives.

balance

When you're gripping it naturally, a well-balanced knife should feel neither handle heavy nor blade heavy. If anything, it should tilt ever so slightly toward the blade rather than the handle.

flexibility

Most types of knives won't flex at all, at least not in a way that you can detect, but for the few that do, such as fillet and boning knives, ask yourself if the amount of give feels appropriate. With bread knives, flexibility is usually a bad sign; you want one that's fairly stiff.

tip **DON'T GET STUCK ON A BRAND: Some knifemakers are known for quality craftsmanship, but you shouldn't buy a knife based on its name alone. It's all about how it feels in your hand, and you won't know that until you start using it.**

buying a set vs. à la carte

WHEN YOU'RE ON A MISSION to purchase several knives at once, you might assume that a package deal is the way to go—more knives at a lower price, right? Not necessarily. It's true that knife sets usually offer a cost savings, selling for less as a unit than if you purchased each item separately. And you get matching handles, if that's your thing. However, sets often include knives that you may not need, such as a utility knife or a tournet knife, so that dilutes their value. And also, it's unlikely that one line offers the best of every knife: The chef's knife might be perfect, but the bread knife might be a little too short. If you do buy a set, go for quality over quantity. A trio of excellent knives is a better value than a mediocre twenty-one-piece set with a "bonus" cutting board. Be sure to put them all through their paces—but give special emphasis to the chef's knife.

If you're serious about putting together a great knife collection, your best bet is to forgo the matched set and buy your knives individually. This way, you can pick the best from each manufacturer, and your collection can grow organically to fit your budget and cooking style (see opposite page). The key to this approach is to resist the impulse to buy everything in one shot. Otherwise, you'll spend way more than you would on a set. So if you can, take it slow. Part of the fun is getting to go back for more.

CREATING A KNIFE SET FROM SCRATCH is as subjective as putting together a wardrobe. Everyone needs a chef's knife and paring knife, but beyond that, your collection should reflect the type of cooking you like to do. The "three-plus-three" strategy here offers one way to build up to an all-purpose and versatile set, but don't hesitate to switch things around for your needs. If you always serve a roast on Sunday, a carving knife should be on your short list. If you do a lot of wok cooking, you may want a vegetable cleaver. Don't overlook a storage system: Get one that will accommodate your expanding collection.

how to build a twelve-piece knife set, three at a time

THE THREE ESSENTIALS

8-inch chef's knife

3½-inch paring knife

9-inch bread knife, ideally with offset handle

ADD THREE MORE

10-inch chef's knife

5½-inch ceramic santoku

Kitchen shears

ADD THREE MORE

4-inch paring knife

9-inch carver

Serrated tomato knife

ADD THREE MORE

Skeleton cheese knife

Boning knife

6-inch chef's knife

cutting boards

AS LONG AS YOU'RE BUYING new knives, go ahead and treat yourself to some new cutting boards. How many do you need? More is better. It's handy to have a variety of sizes for different jobs.

material

Choose either wood, plastic, or a wood fiber composite. Glass, Corian, and acrylic cutting boards ought to be banished—they'll dull your knives in a nanosecond. As a rule, any material that doesn't show scratch marks is probably too hard.

Wooden boards are the kindest to knife edges; they feel great to chop on and their natural look can warm up a kitchen. They're thicker and heavier than plastic, which is a pleasure when you're chopping although a bit of a pain when you have to grab one off a shelf. Maple end-grain boards (recognizable by their checkerboard pattern) are attractive and durable, but costlier than the more typical long-grain boards. Bamboo is beautiful and eco-responsible (it's an easily renewable resource), but it's a bit harder than maple, so your knives may need more frequent honing. A good-quality wooden board that's properly maintained (rub with mineral oil every so often; never let it sit in water) will age nicely, developing a soft patina over time. And if its surface gets marred or deeply scratched, you can always renew it by sanding.

Some people swear by plastic cutting boards. They're safe for knife edges, with polyethylene boards being a bit softer and more prone to deep scratches than polypropylene. Plastic boards are generally less expensive than wood, they're dishwasher safe, and they're lighter and thinner and thus easier to store. Plus, they come in a range of colors, so if you want, you can pick up on your kitchen's color scheme. On the downside, plastic boards, being fairly lightweight, can slide around as you're cutting and when they get covered with scratches, they start to look ratty. Be sure to feel the surface before you buy: A fine-grained pattern is okay, but it can be weird to chop on a board with a nubby texture. You may also come across flexible plastic cutting mats. Some people like these because they're so space efficient and convenient, and you can bend them to funnel food right into the bowl or pan. They can feel flimsy, though, and some of them warp after a few rounds in the dishwasher.

Wood fiber composite boards are a new entry into the cutting board marketplace and within just a few years they've found an enthusiastic following. Although constructed from wood products (one brand bonds together resin-soaked layers of paper), they behave more like plastic: they're thin, lightweight, dishwasher safe, and maintenance free. People who use them seem to love them so if you're looking for something different, you might give one a try.

size and shape

For your primary board, go large. Cutting boards seem to shrink as soon as you start chopping, and it's annoying to feel cramped while prepping. A nice all-purpose size is sixteen by twenty inches, but bigger is even better. Since a large board can be awkward to clean and store, consider giving it a permanent home on your counter. If that's not possible, have an assortment of smaller boards handy for those times when all you need to do is cut a few lemon wedges.

Round and oval boards look pretty, but square and rectangular boards use kitchen space more efficiently. As for thickness, thicker boards are less likely to slide as you cut. They also raise the chopping surface by an inch or so, which you may like, or not.

tip IF YOUR CUTTING BOARD tends to slide around as you chop, take a hint from the pros: Lay a damp paper towel on the counter and set the board on top. The towel prevents slippage.

the eternal debate: wood or plastic?

HAS THIS EVER HAPPENED TO YOU? After slicing raw chicken for a sauté, you wash your wooden board thoroughly and then decide to chop a few tomatoes for a salad. You hope the surface is free of bacteria, but you wonder, is plastic more hygienic than wood? The answer depends on whom you ask. Plastic can be heat sanitized in the dishwasher, but studies have shown that bacteria can survive in deep scratches. Wood can't be sanitized that easily, but it apparently has natural antibacterial properties. What to do? Just choose the material you prefer, and to avoid cross-contamination, designate one of your boards for cutting only raw meat and poultry. If you like the feel of wood, you could set a plastic or silicone cutting mat on the board just for raw meat, then run the mat through the dishwasher.

CUTTING WITH A TRULY SHARP KNIFE can be a revelation. Instead of pushing your knife through the food, you're merely guiding it, so every slice you make is easier, faster, and cleaner. And that makes chopping a whole lot more fun.

But if you walk into the average home kitchen, what you'll find are dull knives. Most people, even many passionate cooks, don't make the effort to keep their knives properly honed and sharpened. Why is this so? Something about the process seems to put people off. Maybe it seems too complicated or scary, or maybe it just feels like too much of a hassle. But sharpening isn't as hard as you think. In fact, it doesn't have to require any skill at all, or even that much time. In a couple of minutes, the job can be done. The key to having sharp knives is this simple: choose the right tool—and then remember to use it.

how to keep them sharp

how sharpening works

BEFORE YOU SETTLE ON A SHARPENING METHOD, it's a good idea to learn a little about knife edges. This section isn't mandatory reading, but if you can visualize what's happening as you're working the edge, you'll be more likely to get good results.

To form the very thin and fine cutting edge of a knife, the blade is beveled to form a V. The angle of this bevel is one of the most important factors in determining a knife's sharpness. The narrower the angle, the thinner the edge and the sharper the knife. At the same time, a narrow bevel is weaker than a wider one and will dull sooner, especially if used to cut through bone or other hard food. Most cooking knives have an angle somewhere between 15 and 23 degrees (measured from the vertical; when both bevels are measured, it's referred to as the "included angle"). Generally speaking, Japanese knives have smaller angles than European-style knives, which hover around 20 or 22 degrees.

The surface polish of the edge also affects sharpness. Even though it looks smooth to the naked eye, the bevel is actually covered with tiny scratches, or microserrations. These serrations can be fine or rough. Knives with a finer, or more polished, finish can be razor sharp and deliver clean, easy cuts, but a little roughness isn't bad because it gives the edge some bite.

As you use your knife, the thin edge wears away. This happens gradually, almost imperceptibly at first, as the microserrations degrade. If you catch this early on, you can correct the edge with just a light tune-up, and the tool for this is a honing steel; this is considered edge maintenance. After a while, though, the edge continues to deteriorate and become truly dull. At this point, the angle is gone, and your blade needs more help than a honing steel can provide. Now you need a sharpener. A knife sharpener grinds away metal from both sides of the edge on an angle, re-creating the bevel and restoring a fine V shape.

The ideal sharpening method for a particular knife depends in part on how far the edge has degraded. Some sharpeners let you grind at only one angle to create a simple V, and if your knife is just a little dull, this will be sufficient. But if you haven't sharpened your knife in a long time, or if you've never sharpened it, the edge is probably not only blunt but thick, so you need to first thin the edge and then set a new angle. The way to do this is by grinding first at a smaller angle and then a wider angle; this creates what's known as a double bevel.

You can get a fairly good sense of the ease and effectiveness of almost any sharpening system if you know two basic things about it: the angle and the abrasive.

> I see cooks who have great knives but they're not sharp. That's like owning a Ferrari and not knowing how to drive.
>
> —Cesare Casella, chef at Maremma

the angle

Maintaining a consistent angle during sharpening is the key to creating a sharp edge. Whether the angle is 16 or 20 degrees isn't nearly as critical as holding the angle constant. If the blade wobbles as you sharpen, you'll get an imperfect edge. Some sharpeners let you choose and hold the angle yourself (to give you more control), and others set and maintain the angle for you (to ensure consistency).

tip CUTTING THROUGH FOOD doesn't dull your knife—your cutting board does. And the harder your knife hits the board, the faster the edge will wear. So lighten up when you cut, and your edge will last a little longer.

the abrasive

To grind metal off the edge, you need an abrasive, which is any material that's harder than the steel blade, such as natural or synthetic stone, diamond, or ceramic. Coarse abrasives remove metal quickly but leave a ragged finish. Finer abrasives remove metal slowly but leave a more polished finish. Some sharpeners have just one type of abrasive, whereas others have multiple abrasives. If your knife is very dull, you might want to start with a coarse abrasive to quickly strip away metal, and then use a smoother abrasive to refine the finish.

what's the difference between maintenance and sharpening?

To *maintain* your edge, use a honing steel. To *sharpen* it, use a sharpener.

A STEEL ...	A SHARPENER ...
Keeps a sharp knife sharp but won't sharpen a dull knife	Sharpens a dull knife
Repairs or restores microserrations along the beveled edge	Re-creates the bevel behind the microserrations
Removes no metal (or imperceptible amounts) from the blade	Shaves metal off the edge
Uses a relatively soft abrasive not much harder than the blade	Uses an abrasive that is much harder than the blade
Should be used frequently to maintain a durable working edge	Should be used only as needed, to avoid excessive wear on the blade

Requires that the knife be held at a steady, consistent angle for optimum results

When you pull your knife out, pull your steel out. Use it every ten or fifteen minutes. If you get in the habit of doing that, you'll maintain the edge of the knife.

—Jody Adams, chef and co-owner of Rialto

FROM LEFT: Wüsthof Interrupted-Diamond diamond steel, Kyocera ceramic sharpening rod, Wüsthof Classic honing steel, Chef's Choice SteelPro pull-through honer, Chantry knife sharpener

maintaining the edge

IT'S IMPORTANT TO HONE the edge of your knife frequently for the same reason that you change the oil in your car. It maintains the edge (and your engine) in good working condition for longer. Regular, proper honing can forestall the need to do major sharpening. The trick—and this is key—is to hone while the knife is still performing well, because by the time you notice that the knife is getting dull, honing is useless. You can stand there honing all day long, but it won't help. So remember, edge maintenance is a preventative measure: It helps keep sharp knives sharp.

honing steels

A honing steel, also called a sharpening steel or a butcher's steel, is a long rod that is often included in knife sets and that, if used correctly, can help maintain your edge. It works by fixing the microserrations along the edge (exactly how it does this is up for debate: some experts insist that it straightens the serrations, but others say it re-creates them). There's consensus on one point, though: You must hold the knife at a very steady angle for the most success when using a steel.

Honing steels come in a variety of sizes. Choose one that is an inch or two longer than your longest knife. The shape isn't crucial. Oval or flat rods may be a smidge more efficient, but round rods work fine, too. The surface may have fine or coarse grooves. Finer grooves will give a more polished edge, but for most cooks, the difference is too subtle to notice. As for material, choose steel for frequent maintenance. It won't strip away metal, at least not that much, so you can use it daily and it won't shorten the life of the blade.

diamond and ceramic steels

Diamond-coated and ceramic steels are often lumped together with steel honing rods, but they're actually a bit different. Since diamond and ceramic are considerably harder than the steel used to make knives, they can abrade metal from the edge and create a new bevel—in other words, they sharpen as well as hone. If honing your knives daily or even weekly isn't realistic for you, a diamond-coated or ceramic steel is a good alternative.

WHEN HONING ON A STEEL ROD, good results depend on holding a super-steady angle, and that can take some practice. For a more foolproof device, try the Edgecraft Steel Pro or the Chantry knife sharpener. These both guide the knife along steel rods at a set angle, eliminating the guesswork. Although they do resemble some knife sharpeners, these products are meant for honing, so if you buy one, keep it handy and use it often.

honing made easy

Pull it out every few months or so, or anytime the edge on one of your knives has lost some of its luster, and with a few well-controlled strokes (it's important to maintain the steady angle), you'll be back in business.

tip WHETHER IT'S OUT OF FORGETFUL-NESS OR LAZINESS, most people, even those who know better, don't use a steel as often as they should (which is daily, or at least weekly). As a reminder, keep the rod in a visible, accessible spot, near your knives or your main prep area. The best time to hone is just before a chopping session.

ONLY IN A BAD DREAM will all the knives in your kitchen go totally blunt overnight. In real life, your edges wear gradually. And depending on how dull your knife is, different sharpeners will be more or less effective. Here are tips to help you choose the appropriate tool.

the spectrum of dullness

IF YOUR KNIFE IS FAIRLY SHARP, try using a honing steel to bring it back to peak performance. Or use the last stage on an electric sharpener, or a very fine-grit sharpening stone.

IF YOUR KNIFE IS A LITTLE DULL, you could use a manual sharpener or a diamond-coated sharpening steel. Or, use the medium-abrasive stage on an electric sharpener or a medium-grit sharpening stone.

IF YOUR KNIFE IS TOTALLY BLUNT, you could bring it to a professional sharpener or use a coarse-grit sharpening stone. Or, use the coarsest abrasive slot on an electric sharpener. A manual sharpener with a coarse stage and adjustable angles may also work.

how to use a honing steel

IF YOU'VE NEVER USED A STEEL, take your time with it. Don't be a show-off by taking rapid-fire swipes while holding the rod out in front of you—you'll never maintain a consistent angle. Instead, try this approach.

1 Hold the steel vertically and anchor the tip on a board or towel. Set the heel of the knife (the part nearest the handle) near the top of the steel, angling the blade about 20 degrees off the vertical. (For Japanese-style knives, aim for 16 degrees.) To find 20 degrees, first set the knife edge perpendicular to the steel (that's 90 degrees), then halve it (that's 45 degrees), and then halve it again (that's 22½ degrees). The handle guard on some steels gives a 20-degree angle when you set the flat of the blade against it.

2 Pull the blade toward you while sliding the edge down the steel, applying light pressure. Focus on maintaining the angle, and don't worry about speed. Repeat the stroke on the other side of the blade. Don't change hands. Repeat five or ten more times, always alternating sides. Check the edge (feel it carefully with your finger, or else cut with it). If you're not satisfied, continue steeling.

sharpening options

WHETHER YOU WANT TO BE TOTALLY HANDS OFF or completely hands on or somewhere in between, there's a sharpening method out there for you. Every approach has pros and cons, and the best method will be the one that's most motivating to you. The first step is to decide whether to hire a pro or do it yourself. As you weigh the options, think about how much time you want to spend sharpening and how much control you want over the process. Also consider how dull you tend to let your knives become, how often you intend to sharpen, and how keen an edge you want.

professional sharpening services

If you want nothing to do with the sharpening process, your choice is clear: Pay someone else to do it for you. Skilled professional sharpeners can not only sharpen your knives, they can also repair any damage. If it's necessary, they should be able to thin out the blade, correct its profile, remove chips, and reshape broken tips—all tricky things to do yourself.

Sharpeners' fees vary widely. Some charge by the inch or type of knife, others have a flat per-knife fee, but either way, servicing a full set of knives every six months or so can get costly. There's also the inconvenience factor: You'll be without your knives for a few days. If you don't have time to do the drop-off and pick up, consider a mail-order sharpening service. If sending knives through the mail gives you the willies, look for a service that will ship you packing material and prepaid shipping labels, making the whole operation as easy as returning a Netflix movie.

SHARPNESS ISN'T EASY to measure objectively, so how do you know when your knife is sharp enough? Easy—just use it and see if it's performing as you'd like. If that's not practical, try one of the following tests.

SLICE A TOMATO. A super-sharp knife will glide through the skin and flesh as if there's nothing there.

SLICE A LEMON. The knife should penetrate the rind with ease.

judging sharpness

CUT A SHEET OF PAPER. Hold the sheet in the air and, starting at the top edge, take a slice down toward the bottom edge. The knife should cut cleanly into the paper. If it's very sharp, you may be able to "carve" out curves in the paper.

FEEL THE EDGE–CAREFULLY. A sharp knife will grab a bit if you pull your thumb gently across the side of the blade, moving from the spine toward the edge (don't slide lengthwise down the blade, or you'll cut yourself).

if sharp knives make you nervous…

SOME HOME COOKS say they're reluctant to keep their knives sharp because they don't trust themselves, or perhaps their children, to use them safely. That's a reasonable concern, but you needn't be scared of sharp knives. You just have to be smart with them: Store them securely, handle them attentively, and take good care when cutting. On the other hand, there are degrees of sharpness, and an insanely sharp edge isn't a necessity for everyone. If your fear of getting hurt overshadows everything else, then you'll probably be happiest keeping your knives functionally sharp, rather than razor sharp.

Don't assume that anyone who hangs up a knife-sharpening sign is going to do quality work. It's disappointing, but unfortunately not that unusual, to get your knives back and discover they're not as sharp as you know they can be. Another risk is that some professionals use machines that can overheat the blade or grind off excessive amounts of metal, which if done repeatedly will shorten its life.

But excellent sharpeners do exist. To find one in your area, do some networking: Chat with local chefs or ask your cooking-minded friends (those with sharp knives) for leads. Kitchen and cutlery shops are often a better choice than hardware stores or roadside stands. Before settling on someone, ask some questions to get a sense of his approach.

- Can you see a knife that he has sharpened? The entire edge should be evenly and sufficiently sharp. If the knife has a thick bolster, there should be no notch at the heel. The side of the blade should not have scratches.

- Can he sharpen to a specific angle? A conventional 20- or 22-degree bevel is fine, unless you're dead set on keeping the 16-degree angle on your Japanese-style knife. In that case, the sharpener should be able to accommodate you.

- On very dull knives, will he thin the edge before setting the final angle? That gives a stronger and more durable edge.

- How does he finish the edge? A finer finish (sometimes called a mirror polish) takes more time and may mean that he cares very much about results.

- Does he seem to have a one-size-fits-all approach, or does he assess each knife individually? A good sharpener will examine the knife before he starts working on it and will modify his approach accordingly.

- Does the sharpening equipment produce sparks? Most experts say that high heat can weaken the blade by causing the steel to go out of temper.

tip HOW OFTEN DO YOU NEED TO SHARPEN? A lot depends on how well you care for it (especially how frequently you hone), but if you're a passionate home cook—you make most meals from scratch and entertain often—a quality knife should give you six months to a year of faithful service before it needs serious sharpening.

CLOCKWISE FROM TOP: Lansky gourmet V-style knife sharpener, Füri pull-through, Wüsthof pull-through, Shun sharpening stone

SHUN
WHETSTONE

KAI
DM-0600
White:Grit 6000
Brown:Grit 1000
MADE IN JAPAN

do it yourself

You don't need to be blessed with the handiness gene to effectively sharpen your own knives. From manual devices to electric models to whetstones, sharpeners come in every price range and for all skill levels. Don't fret too much about which one is best—most sharpeners can do a respectable job—and instead focus on finding one that suits your style so you'll be more likely to use it.

manual sharpeners

Most manual sharpeners are quick to use, reasonably priced, and require no special skills or coordination—they almost always have built-in angle guides. They can be fairly effective as long as your blade isn't terribly dull. This is a large category and designs vary quite a bit, but of those you're likely to come across, there are two main styles worth considering:

PULL-THROUGH SHARPENERS feature a set of abrasives that meet at a fixed angle, forming a V. To sharpen the blade, you hold the sharpener steady with one hand and pull the knife through the V slot several times.

Most have one angle setting, but keep your eyes out for those that allow you to customize the angle.

V-STYLE STICK SHARPENERS use abrasive rods or sticks set into a base at a specific angle. Once you understand the concept, these sharpeners make sense and are easy to use. To sharpen a knife, you draw the blade down the side of the stick, almost as though it was a honing steel. Since the abrasive is set on a diagonal, all you have to do to maintain the angle is keep the knife vertical throughout the stroke. Some models have adjustable angles and abrasives.

A third style of manual sharpener is a rudimentary handheld gadget that you pull over the edge of the blade. If you run across this type of product—they're occasionally sold in hardware shops or on sporting-knife Web sites—don't buy it. The tungsten carbide abrasive is quite basic, and it often leaves a rough finish; this is not a tool you want to use on a fine knife. Also, using the sharpener puts your hand perilously close to the knife edge, so these aren't the safest sharpeners around.

SHOULD YOU BUY THE SAME BRAND SHARPENER AS YOUR KNIVES? It's up to you. Are you the type who returns your car to the dealership for an oil change, or do you drive up to the nearest lube shop? Most sharpeners work fine on any brand and type of knife (except serrated blades and chisel-ground Japanese knives). However, it's also true that companies tend to design their sharpeners with their own knives in mind—the Shun electric sharpener, for example, has the ideal angle and abrasives for Shun knives—so you can't go wrong sticking with the same brand as your knife.

brand loyalty

FROM TOP: Chef's Choice Model 120 electric 3-stage knife sharpener, Shun electric knife sharpener

electric sharpeners

Electric sharpeners are fast, convenient, effective, and easy to use. Just plug the device in, turn it on, and draw the knife through the slots (one slot for each side of the knife) while an abrasive disk spins against the edge. The angle is fixed. They're fairly versatile, able to sharpen knives at different stages of dullness. On the negative side, they're heavier and bulkier than most manual sharpeners, so they don't store as easily. But maybe that's okay, as it's handy to keep the appliance on the counter for the occasional touch-up. They're also noisy, and even though the sharpening goes quickly (thirty to forty-five seconds per knife), it's not the most pleasant listening experience.

Chef's Choice dominates the electric sharpener market, with several models for home cooks. Each one has a different combination of abrasives and angles, and you can make yourself crazy trying to figure out how they differ. Price can help you decide, but if you're looking for one all-purpose electric sharpener, consider the Model 120. It has three stages of abrasives, and the angle changes slightly with each stage, creating a durable triple bevel. The first-stage abrasive is a coarse-grit diamond, meant for only the dullest knives—you needn't draw the blade through more than once or twice. The second stage uses a finer-grit diamond. If your knives are only a little dull, begin sharpening with this stage. The third stage, called stropping, uses a flexible plastic disk with very fine abrasives to polish the edge. This stage removes virtually no metal; you can treat it like a honing steel, using it as frequently as you want to maintain the edge.

The Chef's Choice Model 130 sharpener is similar to the 120, except the second stage uses a steel abrasive, which is meant to give the edge a little bite. Both models can sharpen serrated knives or traditional Japanese knives beveled on one side only.

You can sharpen contemporary double-beveled Japanese-style knives on any electric sharpener, but to restore the original narrow angle, you'll need a model that's designed especially for Asian knives. Chef's Choice and Shun both make one.

SERRATED KNIVES STAY SHARP LONGER than straight-edge knives, partly because the inside of the scallops never touch the hard board—the teeth see most of the action. Once they do get dull, though, the sharpening options are limited. With a few exceptions, most manual sharpeners cannot handle a serrated edge—Spyderco's V-style stick sharpener is one of the exceptions. Some electric sharpeners can repair the teeth, but not the inside of the scallops. If you don't have either of those tools, and if it's a quality knife, your best bet is to have it professionally sharpened by a service that has the necessary equipment. Or, you could take the disposable approach. Buy an inexpensive serrated knife, use it until it's no good, then toss it out (or recycle it) and buy another.

sharpening serrated knives

WHEN SHOPPING FOR A MANUAL OR ELECTRIC SHARPENER, ask the retailer to explain the strengths and weaknesses of specific models. Some questions to ask: Is the sharpener intuitive to use? How durable is it? (Be aware that ceramic rods can break easily.) Does it fold up when not in use or have a carrying case? For something you'll only need a few times a year, compact storage is a plus. Ask about the angle, the abrasive, and the number of stages, and while you're at it, ask if you can test-drive a sharpener (bring along a dull knife).

what to look for in a sharpener

WHAT'S THE ANGLE? Most models don't reveal their preset angle, although they might obliquely refer to having "the ideal angle." That probably means about 20 degrees or a tiny bit more, as that's widely considered the optimum for European knives. A sharpener with adjustable angles is a good thing, as it lets you customize the edge if you want. If you have a Japanese-style knife, look for a sharpener that says it's specifically for Asian knives. That's a clue that it sharpens at a smaller angle.

WHAT'S THE ABRASIVE? The type of abrasive can suggest how aggressively the sharpener will remove metal and how polished the edge will be. Tungsten carbide and diamond shave off a lot of metal quickly, but in return they leave a rougher finish. Ceramic abrasives grind more slowly and deliver a finer edge. Steel abrasives remove almost no metal—they're meant for final polishing after the real sharpening is done. Or, you can use them instead of a honing steel. Some sharpeners will combine two or more materials in the same unit; the Füri TechEdge system, for example, features a carbide edge restorer, diamond sharpener, and honing steel all in one unit, truly covering both ends of the sharpening spectrum.

HOW MANY STAGES? Sharpeners with two or more stages are more versatile and more effective on duller knives. The first stage has a coarser abrasive, and perhaps also a narrower angle for thinning the edge. Subsequent stages have finer abrasives to smooth the edge. You choose the stage you need—extremely dull knives will need the first stage, and slightly dull knives may only need touching up on the second or third stages.

sharpening stones

Sharpening on a stone is traditional and low-tech. It's just you, your knife, and an abrasive brick—no motor to speed the process, no preset angle to ensure consistency. Fans of this method say that it's gratifying, even relaxing, to retool their edges by hand. They appreciate having total control over the type of abrasive, the angle, and the finish—they can customize and polish their edges to their heart's content. But freehand sharpening isn't easy. It takes concentration, coordination, and hours of practice (some say years) to master. And while you're on the learning curve, stones can be frustrating. Just when you sense that you're getting somewhere, you lose the edge and the knife seems duller than ever. It can be messy, particularly if you lubricate with oil or water. And it's slower than other methods (it can be done in ten or fifteen minutes, but many spend hours at it, painstakingly working their way from the coarsest grit to the finest). There's also the possibility of damaging the blade by improper grinding.

Those caveats aside, some people take to the stone quite naturally. If you're good with your hands and feel drawn to this approach, go ahead and give it a try. If you enjoy it and want to learn more, there are many books and websites devoted to this subject.

Sharpening stones come in a variety of materials.

- Natural abrasives, such as Arkansas stones, are mined from a limited number of quarries, and the best-quality stones are becoming scarcer, driving prices up. Natural stones are revered by some, but the quality can be inconsistent, and they're fragile. They're also porous and work best with a lubricant such as honing oil.

- Diamond stones are actually steel plates impregnated with diamond particles. They're very effective for fast sharpening. They can deliver a good working edge but not a very fine finish. They're not as expensive as you would expect and they should last a lifetime.

- Ceramic stones are not as porous as natural stones, so you can use them without a lubricant. Ceramic can give a very fine polished edge.

- Water stones can create a superfine polished edge, but they require special preparation and maintenance. They must be submerged in water for at least ten minutes before use, and then treated with a "stone fixer" to prevent uneven wear.

The term *grit* is used to describe a stone's coarseness. The grit may be expressed with a number ranging from 100 to 8,000 or higher; lower numbers correspond to a coarser abrasive (similar to sandpaper). But just as often, they're simply labeled descriptively as extra coarse, coarse, medium, and so on. Finer, higher-grit stones sharpen more slowly but leave a more refined finish. You choose the grit based on the condition of your knives and how polished you want the edge. Very blunt knives need a coarser-grit stone to reshape the edge quickly. Then you can use a finer grit to polish it.

tip IN A PINCH, A CERAMIC PLATE can become a makeshift sharpening stone. Flip the plate over and draw the knife edge along the unglazed bottom ring, trying to hold a steady 20-degree angle. This won't give a refined edge, but if you're at, say, your mother-in-law's house where all the knives are desperately dull, this will temporarily restore a working edge. The ring of the plate will turn gray; just swipe it with a sponge and it will clean right up.

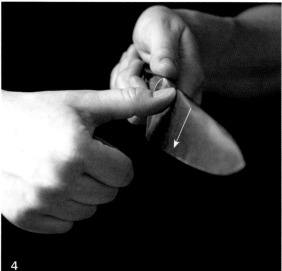

how to use a sharpening stone

THERE ARE MANY TECHNIQUES for and opinions about sharpening on a stone—some people grind in circles whereas others use straight strokes; some grind on one side repeatedly whereas others alternate sides after every stroke—but the goal with all of them is the same: to evenly grind metal off both sides of the blade and restore a fine edge. As long as you can maintain a consistent angle throughout the process (you can buy angle guides to help), you can experiment with whatever sharpening style you want. Here's one approach that works well for beginners.

1 Set the stone on a stable surface, with a towel underneath so it won't slide around. Lubricate the surface with water or oil, if you want. (As you sharpen, steel filings from the knife's edge can clog the stone's pores, and lubricants help the filings float away.) Hold the knife handle and set the heel of the blade on the stone. Put your fingertips on the tip of the blade. Lift the blade off the stone about 20 degrees, or to your desired angle.

2 Keeping your wrists locked, push the blade away from you across the surface of the stone, moving from heel to tip in an arc. Guide the knife by the handle while applying pressure with your fingers on the tip of the blade. It should feel like you're taking a slice off the stone. Do this stroke once.

3 Flip the knife over and sharpen the other side, but this time pull the blade toward you, moving again from heel to tip in an arc. Flip the knife over again, and continue to sharpen, always alternating sides after one stroke.

4 Feel for a burr. Gently pull your thumb across the side of the blade, moving from the spine toward the edge. If the edge feels sharp but rough, you've created a burr. That means you're ready to move to a finer-grit stone.

Keep sharpening on finer-grit stones, feeling for a burr each time. If you're using a very fine stone, the burr may disappear on its own. If it doesn't, remove it by lightly running the knife down the length of a honing steel once on each side of the blade.

> If you invest a lot of money in a knife, you don't take it to the butcher shop where they sharpen it for $3. If you're not ready to sharpen that knife yourself, you shouldn't own it.
>
> —Nancy Oakes, chef-owner of Boulevard restaurant, author of *Boulevard, The Cookbook*

WHEN YOU OWN GREAT KNIVES, it's a shame not to take care of them. Take a few minutes to learn what to do and what not to do, and you'll be one step closer to keeping your kitchen cutlery in good health.

caring for your knives

The knives that everyone in my family uses are in a knife block. The ones that I use are in a box stored on top of the refrigerator. To be perfectly honest, some of my knives at home are dull. That's why I keep the secret stash.

—Jody Adams, chef and co-owner of Rialto

store them right

A KNIFE-STORAGE SYSTEM might be the last thing you want to buy, especially after you've just spent a few hundred bucks on knives, but it's an essential investment. Storing loose knives in a drawer will ruin the fine edge faster than you can imagine. The goal of any knife-storage system is to avoid harm, both to your knives and yourself. Most products are up to that task, so you should just choose the one you like best.

knife blocks

Perhaps because so many knife sets come with them, wooden knife blocks seem to be the default storage system. They do a fine job, but they have drawbacks. They hog counter space; their angular design makes them bulkier than their footprint suggests. They hide the blades, which makes finding the knife you want like playing a round of Concentration. Cleaning inside the knife slots is next to impossible (but it shouldn't be necessary if you wash and dry your knives before putting them away), so if you're the type to clean every last nook and cranny, a block may drive you nuts.

BUYING AND USAGE TIPS: A block with horizontal rather than vertical slots is friendlier to knives because the edges don't contact the wood. If you do get one with vertical slots, it is helpful to insert your knives with the blade facing up, to preserve the edge. Be sure to choose a block not only with enough slots but also with the right-sized slots, plus a few vacancies for future acquisitions. Some contemporary blocks are designed to let you see the blades, a definite plus.

magnet bars

Convenient, inexpensive, and space efficient, magnet bars are favored by many pros. With your knives in plain view, you can see your options and reach for what you want in one efficient motion. As long as you have an empty section of wall, ideally near your main prep area, magnet bars free up precious counter and drawer space (see page x). The exposed blades may make magnet bars look threatening, but if the magnets are strong and the bar is hung appropriately, they are safe. However, if children will be tramping through the kitchen, an easy-to-reach magnet bar isn't the wisest choice.

BUYING AND USAGE TIPS: For added security, look for bars with a double row of extra-strong magnets; restaurant supply shops may carry them. When choosing the length, allow about ½ to 1 inch between blades. When placing a knife on or taking it off the bar, try to avoid knocking the edge against the magnet. To put a knife on the bar, set the spine on the magnet first, and then turn in the edge. To remove the knife, pull the edge out first.

A knife is like a woman. You need to know how to take care of her. You have to be cordial and nice and have respect. I don't know why, but the knife is something sensual.

—Cesare Casella, chef at Maremma

drawer inserts

If counter space is at a premium and wall storage isn't an option, or if you like to keep your cooking tools behind doors, drawer inserts are the answer. Available in a variety of sizes, they let you devote an entire drawer, or just part of it, to knife storage. A few points to consider: Since the blade rests on the wooden frame, inserts can cause the edge to wear faster; some people place the knife in the slot with the edge facing up, but this looks and is dangerous. Also, because you have to open the drawer first, retrieving a knife becomes a two-step procedure. To prevent the insert from sliding around in the drawer, line the drawer with a rubber gripper mat.

edge guards

These inexpensive plastic sheaths are perfect for protecting knives that you use infrequently and that don't fit into your regular storage device. The sheath, which comes in a variety of sizes, covers the entire blade, so you can safely stash the knife in a drawer. If you're traveling with knives or sending them through the mail, edge guards are a must. Look for edge guards with bright colors so it's easy to find them in the clutter of your utensil drawer.

tip **INSERT THE HEEL OF THE KNIFE INTO the slot first and then lower the rest of the blade. Don't push the tip into the side of the protector, because the knife can easily slip.**

YOUR KNIVES WILL LAST LONGER AND STAY SHARPER if you treat them well. Try to resist the urge to use them as a screwdriver, a lever, a pick, or any other task for which they weren't intended. **be nice to your knives**

CLEAN KNIVES PROMPTLY AFTER USE. They'll clean up easier, and the residue from acidic ingredients such as tomatoes and lemons can dull the edge.

USE AN APPROPRIATE CUTTING BOARD, such as wood or plastic. Don't cut on marble, granite, ceramic, glass, or other hard surfaces.

DON'T CUT FROZEN FOODS WITH STRAIGHT-EDGE KNIVES. That's a fast path to ruining the edge.

DON'T USE THE BLADES TO PRY OPEN CANS or otherwise twist the blades.

CLEANING A KNIFE PROPERLY isn't rocket science. Simply wash it with hot soapy water as soon as possible after you use it, dry it with a clean soft towel, and store it in its place.

There's a lot more to say about what *not* to do.

DON'T put knives in the dishwasher. The high heat isn't good for the steel, and the agitation can knock the knife against other utensils, dulling the edge. Dishwashers can also damage wooden handles.

DON'T let knives drip dry in a rack or utensil bucket. In addition to leaving

how to wash a knife

water spots on the knife, this can damage the tip and edge. Just take an extra five seconds to dry the knife and put it away.

DON'T leave dirty knives in the sink overnight. Water and acidic and salty residues on the blade can make the metal, especially the thin edge, vulnerable to rusting.

DON'T use steel wool. This will scratch the blade. Hot soapy water and a sponge will remove any dried-on food particles.

AVOID sliding the sponge lengthwise along the edge of the blade. A very sharp knife could slice through the sponge and nick your hand. Instead, wipe from the spine toward the edge with short, diagonal strokes.

making the cut

PART TWO

THERE'S SOMETHING MESMERIZING about the way a professional chef wields a knife, slicing a carrot into uniform rounds in seconds, and the percussive rat-a-tat-tat of the blade as it taps the board. That kind of speed and precision comes only after years of daily practice, but there are ways to quickly boost your own knife skills without investing a whole lot of time. A little tweak to your grip, a brief lesson on cutting techniques, and you'll be on your way. The payoff? The food you cook will look prettier, it'll taste better, you'll enjoy the prep work more, and you'll feel like a pro. As a bonus, your newfound knife skills will shave a few minutes off the time it takes to get dinner on the table.

knife-skill
fundamentals

how to grip a knife

THE NEXT TIME you pick up a knife, pay attention to how you hold it. Are you clutching the handle like a sword? Is your index finger extended along the spine? It might seem like a small thing, but how you grip the knife can either help or hinder your cutting.

The best grip is the one that makes you feel the most comfortable and secure, and it will vary depending on the type of knife, what you're cutting, the size of your hand, and your own preferences. Not everyone holds a pen the same way, and there's similar variation in how people grasp their knives. But some hand positions offer more control than others, so experiment with the chef's knife and paring knife grips shown here and see if they work for you.

What about other types of knives? In some cases, you can use a variation on these grips (you might hold a vegetable cleaver similarly to a chef's knife), but for the most part, your hand position isn't as crucial. So when it comes to slicers, bread knives, cheese knives, and more, just hold the handle intuitively.

with a chef's knife

Many pros use the "pinch" grip. Choke up on the handle, pinching the blade between your curled index finger and your thumb and wrapping your three back fingers around the handle. This may feel a little precarious at first, but once you get used to it, it can give you a lot of power, control, and precision. If you have small hands or are using a 10-inch chef's knife, choking up like this can help you feel in charge of the knife. The pinch grip also works particularly well with European-style knives because the thick bolster acts as a finger guard. On Japanese-style knives with no bolster, this grip is still effective, although their lighter, thinner blades make them a little easier to maneuver even when your hand is farther back on the handle.

with a paring knife

You need two grips, one for cutting on a board and another for cutting food in your hand.

On the board, try a modified pinch grip, letting your curled index finger rise a bit higher so only the pad of your fingertip touches the blade. Or, you can pull back a bit and wrap all your fingers around the handle.

When using a paring knife off the board, to peel an onion, for example, wrap your fingers around the handle, with your index finger close to or even hugging the spine of the blade (and the fingertip on the side of the blade). Your thumb is free to rest on the object being cut. You may do this naturally when you peel an apple or pear.

For certain tasks, such as coring a tomato or strawberry or removing potato eyes, it helps to choke up on the blade even more, so you're really in control of the tip.

There is a tendency among some home cooks to extend their index finger on the spine of the blade of both paring knives and chef's knives. This isn't necessarily wrong (in fact, Japanese chefs use this grip to fillet fish), but if your knife isn't that sharp, you may end up pressing down on the blade with your finger (rather than pushing forward with your arm, where your strength is). But it's up to you. If you're happy with the cuts you're making and you feel in control of the knife, don't feel obliged to change grips.

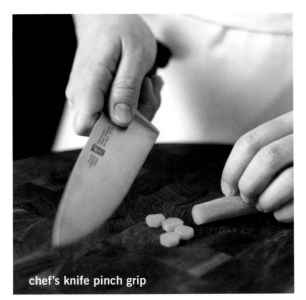

chef's knife pinch grip

paring knife pinch grip

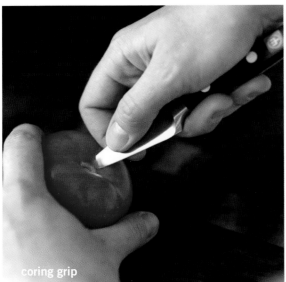

coring grip

peeling grip

the guiding hand

The hand that's not holding the knife, called the guiding hand, works in harmony with your blade. It stabilizes the food and also controls the size of the cut, all while keeping clear of the knife edge. Many home cooks hold the food too casually, making their fingertips easy targets for the descending blade. There's a safer way. Place your hand so the middle fingers face the blade and your thumb and pinkie hang back. Curl your fingers slightly so your knuckle protrudes more than the fingertips. Professionals use their knuckles as a guide for the knife, letting the side of the blade actually tap their knuckles as they slide their hand backward along the food. But if that feels awkward and scary, don't do it. A modified version of the technique works just as well, where you move your guiding hand backward in advance of the blade. Sometimes, your guiding hand plays a different role, such as stabilizing the tip of the knife when chopping herbs.

tip DON'T PUSH THE FOOD TOWARD THE BLADE as you cut; instead, move the knife and your guiding hand along the food.

left-handedness

Lefties go through life tolerating certain injustices—the three-ring binder, for instance, and ladles with the spout on the wrong side—but in terms of kitchen knives, left-handed folks are mostly on equal footing. Conventional knives are beveled symmetrically, so they present no problem. One exception is the traditional single-bevel Japanese knife, which is geared toward righties, with the bevel on the right side of the blade; left-handed versions can be special ordered. Serrated knives are also beveled on the right side only, and this can cause the knife to veer off course when a lefty is slicing, producing uneven slices. It's not a major concern, but if it troubles you, you can find left-handed bread knives online.

With due respect to lefties (I myself am one), the cutting techniques in this chapter are shown from a right-handed perspective. If you're a fellow lefty, this shouldn't be an issue. The cutting instructions are written in an ambidextrous way, and the main purpose of the photos is to see the interplay of the knife and the food. Your hands will naturally follow.

knife safety

EVERY KNIFE IS potentially dangerous, and the best way to avoid injury is simply to remember that fact. As one knife-skills instructor advises her students, "You respect the blade, and the blade respects you." You don't need to be afraid of a sharp knife. You do need to pay attention to what you're doing, use common sense, and follow these tips.

- Be especially vigilant around knives that have recently been sharpened. Your muscles tend to remember the duller edge and maneuver the knife accordingly.

- Keep your eyes on the knife whenever you're cutting or reaching for it. If we all followed this seemingly obvious piece of advice, there would be far fewer knife injuries.

- When you set a knife down on the counter, lay the cutting edge away from you.

- Never set a knife on the counter with the handle protruding off the edge. It's too easy to bump the handle and send the knife spinning.

- Never test a knife's sharpness by sliding your finger along the blade.

- Set up your cutting area so other people won't get in your way.

- Never try to catch a falling knife. This sounds self-evident, but the natural impulse is to grab for a falling object.

- Don't put a knife into a sink full of soapy water, or a sink that will be filled with water. You should always be able to see the blade.

- Be careful when walking with a knife in hand. The rule in restaurant kitchens is to hold it with the tip toward the floor, the cutting edge facing your thigh, and your arm stiff—not a bad idea for home, too.

- When handing someone a knife, offer the handle, not the blade. Even better, set the knife down on a surface and let the other person pick it up.

- If you have small children, store your knives in a secure place out of their reach. Keep children a safe distance away while cutting. Don't leave a knife near the edge of a counter, where inquisitive, groping hands can grab it.

is a sharp knife safer? (no!)

HAVE YOU EVER HEARD THE SAYING that a dull knife is more dangerous than a sharp one? This bit of folklore may have a kernel of truth to it: you use more force with a dull knife, and if it slips, it can be bad news. But knife mishaps happen in countless other ways and, quite frankly, most of the time a sharp knife is involved, simply because it cuts so easily and deeply, even if your skin barely glances the edge. Nevertheless, knife experts and cooking pros keep repeating the adage (perhaps they're hoping to frighten people into sharpening?). So let's be honest: a very sharp knife is *more* likely to cause injury than a dull one. Don't get me wrong. A well-honed knife is a wonderful thing, but you must always be on guard while using it.

Two things are fundamental. One, if you're using a knife, you're focused on the knife. Period. There should be no distractions. Second, you need to practice. It's not hard. Just buy a bag of potatoes and practice making julienne and brunoise. If you focus and you're not in a rush, you'll get it. Then you boil it all up and make some mashed potatoes.

—Ming Tsai, host and executive producer of
Simply Ming, and chef-owner of Blue Ginger

cutting motions

YOU CAN MOVE A KNIFE in three directions in order to cut: You can push forward, pull backward, or press downward. Usually a combination of forward slicing plus slight downward pressure works fine, but sometimes a different stroke works even better.

locomotive

For most chopping with a chef's knife, a combination of a forward push with slight downward pressure efficiently moves the blade through the food. Do this repeatedly, and the movement of your arm resembles the wheels on a locomotive. This motion is also called the rock-chop because you're rocking the knife back and forth as you chop.

forward-backward combination

A sawing motion with minimal downward pressure—just long forward and backward strokes—works best with serrated knives. This lets you cut into foods that are tougher outside than they are inside, such as a to- mato or loaf of bread, to avoid crushing the interior. It's also the best stroke for slicing cooked meat, such as a roast, ham, or turkey breast.

backward

When you're cutting raw fish or meat, pull- ing the knife backward means there's less chance that the tip will puncture or shear the flesh. Sushi chefs always use long backward strokes. When boning chicken breast or thighs, short backward swipes with the knife allow for more precise cuts.

push-cut

A straight downward cut is technically the least efficient (most knives cut better with some forward or backward motion), but sometimes it does the trick. Use it to cut soft cheeses such as chèvre and Brie, to cut slices of pizza or a tart without disrupting the topping, to halve a winter squash or slice a carrot lengthwise, to chop herbs or sever cartilage or bone.

tip **TO MAKE A MODERATELY DULL KNIFE** feel a little sharper than it is, use longer strokes and less downward pressure. This changes the angle of attack on the food, multiplying the effectiveness of microserrations along the cutting edge.

DOWN THE LEFT: mince, chop, chiffonade
DOWN THE RIGHT: large dice, medium dice, small dice, brunoise

basic cuts, defined

WHEN FOLLOWING A RECIPE, you're constantly instructed to "dice" or "mince" or "chop" ingredients, but it's not always clear exactly how big or small the cut should be. The type and size of the cut can affect everything from how quickly the ingredient cooks to how it tastes (minced cilantro tastes a little different from coarsely chopped), so it's not an arbitrary decision. Usually the goal is to end up with pieces of all the same size and shape. This isn't merely for aesthetics: Evenly sized pieces cook at the same rate. The following are standard definitions of several common cuts, which derive from classic French culinary techniques (thus the French terms). In the next chapters, you'll learn how to execute these cuts on specific vegetables.

dice

Dicing is cutting food into uniformly sized cubes. There are no firm rules on when to use each size, but keep in mind that a smaller dice cooks faster and integrates more with the rest of the dish.

LARGE DICE: ¾-inch cubes

MEDIUM DICE: ½-inch cubes

SMALL DICE: ¼-inch cubes

BRUNOISE (broo-nwahz): ⅛-inch cubes

mince

Mincing is an even, very fine cut with tiny pieces too small to be easily measured. Herbs, garlic, ginger, and other flavorings are often minced. The finer you chop these ingredients, the more they will flavor and meld with other ingredients in the dish.

chiffonade

This cut is primarily used to slice fresh large-leafed herbs such as basil and mint into thin ribbons, often used as a garnish.

chop

The words *chopping* and *dicing* are often used interchangeably—for most vegetables, the same technique can be used for both cuts—but technically, chopping implies less precision and uniformity. While a large or small dice usually refers to a specific dimension, a coarse or fine chop can be more ambiguous. Chopping is appropriate when you're making braises and stews, pureed soups, or any other dish where the size and shape of the vegetable isn't critical. If a recipe says to "coarsely chop" an ingredient, don't bother pulling out a ruler. Just cut larger pieces of roughly the same size. Ideally, the recipe will offer some guidance, but if there's no indication whatsoever (as in, "1 onion, chopped"), you might aim for something close to a medium dice. Chopping also applies to ingredients that are too small or uneven to dice, such as herbs, garlic, capers, or nuts.

slice

Sliced ingredients have a lot of surface area relative to their thickness, so they cook quickly and can develop lots of flavorful caramelization. On cylindrical foods such as carrots or a baguette, cutting straight across produces rounds (or *rondelles*), whereas cutting on a diagonal, or on the bias, produces bigger oblong slices. On thin vegetables such as asparagus, a sharp diagonal cut exposes more surface area for extra browning and absorption of sauces.

julienne

These are long, rectangular strips of a certain thickness. The length is variable. As with slices, this cut exposes a lot of surface area for quick cooking and ample browning.

BATONNET: ¼ by 2 to 3 inches

JULIENNE: ⅛ by 1 to 2½ inches (also called matchsticks, or allumettes, when referring to potatoes)

FINE JULIENNE: ¹⁄₁₆ by 1 to 2½ inches

what about wedges?

Although they're not considered a standard cut, wedges are a common way to prepare round vegetables and fruit. When a recipe refers to the size of a wedge, measure the widest point on the rounded side. To cut a potato, beet, apple, peach, or anything else into wedges, start by cutting it in half. Then set the flat side down and cut through the rounded side, tilting the blade as necessary to get even wedges. Keeping the flat side down is safer and gives you more control over the size of the wedge (see page 113).

---

size matters

WHEN YOU'RE IMPROVISING A DISH, there comes a point where you have to decide how to cut the food. Will you mince or julienne the ginger? Cube or wedge the potato? Here are some points to consider as you make up your mind.

BALANCE: It's pleasing to have evenly sized ingredients in a dish (such as a chopped salad or salsa), but if you want one ingredient to be the star, cut it larger than the rest.

PREP TIME: The finer the cut, the longer it takes to prep. It's quicker and less fussy to cut a potato into wedges than into a dice.

COOKING TIME: The smaller and thinner you cut an ingredient, the faster it will cook. Sliced beets roast faster than large chunks.

FLAVOR INTEGRATION: Smaller cuts meld with the rest of the dish. If you want the garlic to really infuse your sauce, mince rather than chop.

APPEARANCE: Sometimes the cut won't affect the final look of a dish—in a puréed soup, for example—but usually it does. Changing the cut is an easy way to perk up the same old recipes. The next time you roast some vegetables, try a julienne cut instead of wedges or cubes.

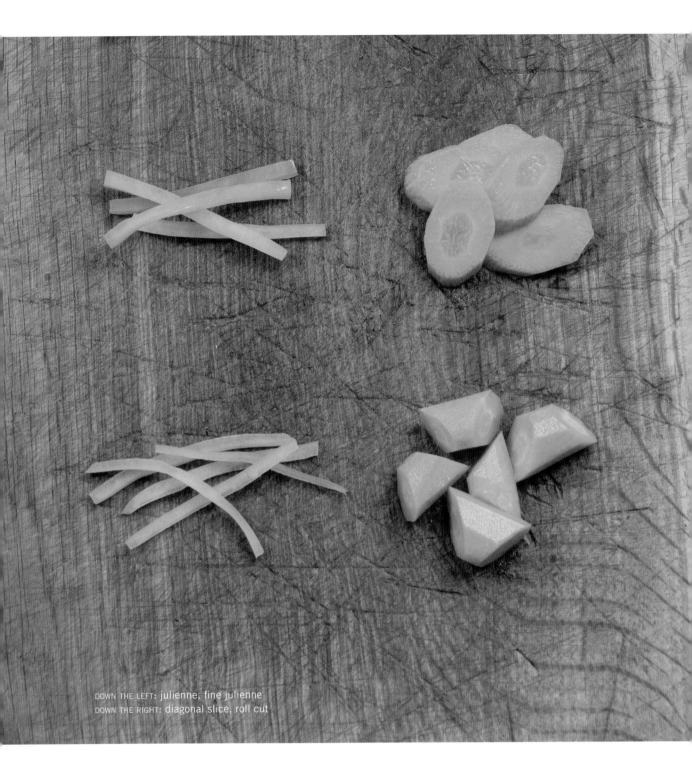

DOWN THE LEFT: julienne, fine julienne
DOWN THE RIGHT: diagonal slice, roll cut

IN THE KITCHEN, just as in life, there's never only one right way to do something. Many paths can lead you to a uniform dice of eggplant or neatly sliced apple, and if your own approach is working well, you needn't change it. However, if you tend to be a little disordered or random with your chopping, you'll find the techniques here quite helpful. Practice them when you can, and soon enough they'll become second nature. Use your chef's knife in all cases, unless the method specifies another type of knife.

vegetables, fruit, and more

onions

trimming and peeling

Trim off the end opposite the hairy root. Cut the onion in half through the root. Using a paring knife, grab a corner of the cut edge and peel off and discard the papery outer skin.

slicing crosswise semicircles

The crosswise cut is quick and produces concentric semicircles of various sizes. Set one onion half flat side down. Cut crosswise slices of the width you need. When you approach the root, flip the onion onto its other flat side (so you have a wider base), and continue slicing. Repeat with the other onion half.

slicing lengthwise slices (radial cut)

This lengthwise cut produces uniform crescents that will cook a bit more evenly. The trick with this cut is to angle the knife so you're cutting toward the center of the onion, almost like making spokes on a wheel; this is sometimes called a radial cut.

1 Set one onion half flat side down. Position the knife just above the root, and notch out the entire root core using a diagonal cut and discard it. (Removing the whole core allows the slices to separate.) Starting on one end of the onion and tilting the blade so it's almost parallel to the board, cut a couple of lengthwise (longitudinal) slices, cutting through to the center of the onion.

2 Continue slicing, raising the knife as you follow the curve of the onion, always cutting to the center. When you're at the halfway point, the knife should be completely vertical.

3 Turn the onion onto its other flat side. Repeat the cut, taking your time with the last few slices, when you're left with a very narrow wedge—it helps to pinch the wedge between your thumb and index finger, carefully insert the knife, and slice down.

dicing and mincing

To vary the size of the dice, just change the width of the cuts. You can use this "grid method" to dice shallots and garlic, too; use a paring knife.

1 Start by halving the onion through the root and peeling the skin. Set one onion half cut side down. Orient the blade so it's parallel to the board, and bunch your fingers on top of the onion (or lay your hand flat on the onion, with fingers slightly arched). Make two or three horizontal cuts through the onion, but don't cut through to the root (it holds the onion together).

2 Using the tip of the knife, cut a series of evenly spaced vertical slices from the root end to the tip, again leaving the root intact.

3 Now, cut across the onion at the same width as your previous cuts, creating a dice.

4 To mince the onions, gather them into a rough pile. With your hand on the tip of the knife, use and up-and-down motion to chop from one side of the pile to the other, letting the tip of the knife act as a pivot point. Periodically stop to slide any pieces off the blade and gather the onions into a pile. Continue chopping and gathering until the mince is as fine as you need.

shallots

mincing

You can dice, slice, and mince shallots just as you do onions, except use a paring knife since shallots are smaller. If the shallot has two lobes, separate them and set each lobe on its flatter side. If it's a single oblong or round shallot, halve it lengthwise through the root, just as you would for an onion.

caramelized onion tart with kalamata olives

Served with a simple salad, this makes a lovely light supper. Cut into smaller squares, it becomes an enticing hors d'oeuvre. The onion slicing takes a few minutes, but when you're done, you'll have the radial cut down pat.

SERVES 8 AS AN APPETIZER, 4 AS A LIGHT MAIN COURSE

1 pound (about 4) yellow onions, cut into ¼-inch-thick lengthwise slices

3 tablespoons extra-virgin olive oil

¼ teaspoon kosher salt

1¼ teaspoons fresh rosemary

1 sheet frozen puff pastry (9 ounces), thawed overnight in the fridge or at room temperature for 45 minutes (keep refrigerated until ready to use)

6 to 8 pitted kalamata olives, halved lengthwise

4 to 6 anchovy fillets (optional)

PREHEAT the oven to 400°F. Line a baking sheet with parchment paper.

WITH a chef's knife, cut the onions into ¼-inch-thick lengthwise slices using the radial cut (see page 95); you should have about 4 cups of onions.

HEAT the oil in a 12-inch skillet over medium heat. Add the onions and salt, and cook, stirring often and adjusting the heat as needed, until the onions are caramelized, about 35 minutes; they should be soft and darkened to a golden shade of tan. You may need to add a bit of water to the pan to prevent sticking.

ADD 1 teaspoon of the rosemary and season with salt to taste. Transfer the onions to a plate and let cool to lukewarm, at least 15 minutes.

MEANWHILE, prepare the dough. Gently unfold the sheet of puff pastry on a lightly floured surface. Mend any cracks in the seams by pinching the dough together. Roll out the dough to an 11-inch square. Lift it gently and set it on the prepared pan. Prick the dough with a fork in several places (but not the rim). Refrigerate the dough until you're ready to assemble the tart.

DISTRIBUTE the onions evenly over the dough (tuck in any strands that extend beyond the square, or they'll burn). Arrange the olives evenly on top. If using, lay the anchovies between the olives. Bake until the crust is golden on top and underneath all the way into the center (lift it up to check), 20 to 25 minutes.

TRANSFER the tart to a cutting board. Sprinkle the remaining ¼ teaspoon rosemary on the tart. Use a chef's knife to cut straight down through the crust and portion the tart into squares. Serve warm.

garlic

THE GREEN SPROUT inside mature garlic cloves can be bitter, so if you want, pry it out with the tip of a paring knife after halving the garlic.

chopping and mincing

For tiny, even cubes of garlic, you could use a paring knife and the grid technique (shown on an onion on page 96), but it's a tedious job on more than one or two cloves. Here's a faster method.

1   Trim the root end of the clove. Set the flat side of a chef's knife on the unpeeled garlic clove and press firmly on the blade with the heel of your hand to smash the clove. The skin should loosen so it's easier to remove.

2   Chop the garlic very coarsely.

3   With your hand on the tip of the knife and using a straight up-and-down motion, chop from one side of the pile to the other, letting the tip of the knife act as a pivot point. Continue until the pieces are as finely chopped or minced as needed.

cutting slivers

Peel and trim the garlic clove and slice it lengthwise. Fan the slices and then make lengthwise cuts to get thin strips.

pureeing

Mashing garlic to a paste delivers pungent flavor without affecting the texture of a sauce or dish—ideal for aioli, dressings, or marinades. For large quantities, use a food processor or mortar and pestle, but for just a couple of cloves, use a chef's knife.

Mince the garlic as finely as possible as shown on opposite page. Sprinkle a good pinch of kosher salt over the garlic (for friction). Angling the blade so it's nearly parallel to the board, scrape the knife sideways over the garlic repeatedly until it's pureed, pressing on the side of the blade more than the cutting edge.

classic caesar salad with garlic croutons

The raw egg yolk emulsifies the dressing so it is creamy and rich, but if you're concerned about serving uncooked eggs, either use pasteurized whole eggs, now available in some supermarkets, or else omit the yolk entirely. Focaccia or ciabatta make pleasantly toothsome croutons; if they're not available, English muffins are an excellent alternative. If you've never pureed garlic with the side of a chef's knife, here's your chance.

SERVES 4 AS A LIGHT SUPPER

CROUTONS

4 slices bacon (5 ounces), cut crosswise into thin strips

1 clove garlic

2 tablespoons extra-virgin olive oil

6 (½-inch) slices focaccia or ciabatta, cut into ½-inch cubes (about 3 cups)

Kosher salt

DRESSING

1 clove garlic

¼ teaspoon kosher salt

3 anchovy fillets

1 large egg yolk

2 tablespoons fresh lemon juice

1 teaspoon Dijon mustard

¼ cup extra-virgin olive oil

3 tablespoons loosely packed grated Parmigiano-Reggiano cheese

Freshly ground black pepper

10 large romaine lettuce leaves (preferably from the heart), washed and spun dry (about 12 cups)

Shavings of Parmigiano-Reggiano cheese, for garnish

TO make the croutons, set the bacon in a medium skillet over medium-low heat, and cook, stirring occasionally, until crisp, about 7 minutes. Transfer the bacon to a plate; leave the fat in the pan and the burner on medium-low.

SMASH and peel the garlic (see page 100). Add the oil and garlic to the skillet and let sizzle until the garlic is light golden, 1 to 2 minutes. Spoon out the garlic and discard it. Increase the heat to medium, add the bread, and season with a big pinch or two of salt. Toast the bread, tossing the pieces frequently until golden brown on a few sides, about 4 minutes. Remove the pan from the heat and set aside. (This yields more croutons than you'll need, so it's okay to munch a few.)

TO make the dressing, mash the garlic and salt to a smooth puree using the side of a chef's knife (see page 101). Scrape the puree into a small bowl. Mash the anchovy fillet to a paste the same way and add it to the bowl. Add the egg yolk, lemon juice, and mustard to the bowl and whisk to blend. Gradually drizzle in the olive oil, whisking constantly to maintain the emulsion. Add the grated cheese and a few grinds of pepper and stir to combine.

CUT or tear the lettuce across the ribs into large bite-size pieces. Put them in a large wooden salad bowl. Drizzle about three-quarters of the dressing on top and toss. The leaves should be just lightly coated; if needed, drizzle on the rest of the dressing. Add the croutons and bacon, and toss. Sprinkle the cheese shavings on the salad, plus a few grinds of black pepper, and serve.

bread-and-butter pudding with rum and crystallized ginger

Even people who aren't fans of bread pudding sing the praises of this one. The warmth of the ginger infuses the custard while adding a little zing to each bite. To keep crystallized ginger (and other sticky ingredients such as dried fruit) from sticking to your knife, coat the knife with a very light film of vegetable oil or spray. Demerara and turbinado sugars are becoming increasingly available in supermarkets, but if you can't find either one, any sugar with larger crystals will do, or even regular granulated sugar. A good-quality serrated knife makes quick work of cubing the bread.

SERVES 6 TO 8

4 tablespoons unsalted butter, softened

1 (12-ounce) loaf day-old Italian bread, cut into 1-inch-thick slices

4 large eggs

2½ cups whole milk

1½ cups heavy cream

¾ cup granulated sugar

1 teaspoon vanilla extract

1 teaspoon dark rum

Big pinch of kosher salt

⅓ cup coarsely chopped crystallized ginger

2 teaspoons turbinado sugar, or other coarse sugar

PREHEAT the oven to 350°F.

SPREAD the butter on one side of each bread slice. Cut each slice into 1-inch strips and then crosswise into 1-inch cubes using a serrated knife. You should have about 12 cups. Set aside.

COMBINE the eggs, milk, cream, sugar, vanilla, rum, and salt in a very large bowl. Whisk just until blended. Add the bread and toss gently just until all the cubes are thoroughly coated. Sprinkle on the ginger and stir gently to combine. Pour the mixture into an 8-cup baking dish (7 by 11-inch works well), spreading it evenly; the pudding will fill the pan to the rim. Let stand for 10 minutes, pressing the top layer of bread with the back of a large spoon every few minutes.

SPRINKLE the turbinado sugar evenly over the bread. Bake until the pudding has puffed, the top and bottom are light golden brown, and a knife inserted into the center comes out hot, 60 to 65 minutes. Remove from the oven and let cool for at least 10 minutes. Serve warm.

ginger

peeling

First, trim off any protruding knobs and bumps from the portion of ginger you intend to use. To peel ginger without losing too much of the underlying flesh, scrape off the skin with a small spoon. The spoon maneuvers around the knobs a little easier than a peeler, and it removes only the dry outer skin. Alternatively, use the back of a paring knife. Cut off the peeled section from the rest of the root.

julienning and mincing

Ginger's stringy fibers run lengthwise, so it's a little easier to cut first with the fibers to make thin slices, and then across the grain to mince.

1 Cut a very thin slice lengthwise from one side and set the ginger on the flat base.

2 Cut the ginger into thin lengthwise slices (with the grain).

3 Shingle the slices so they partially overlap one another and cut them lengthwise into long, thin strips (or julienne).

4 Gather the julienned ginger together and cut across the strips into fine dice or mince.

leeks

trimming the top

Before cutting up a leek, you need to trim off the thick dark green upper leaves. But don't just lop them off with one crosswise cut. That sacrifices the lighter and more tender green leaves that continue higher up the inner stalk. Instead, cut away one layer at a time. It's fussier but worth it. If you want, freeze the dark green trimmings for making broth.

1 Make a shallow cut into the outer dark green leaf right at the spot where the leaf becomes lighter. Remove the leaf to expose the next layer, trimming it the same way.

2 Continue removing layers and rotating the leek, moving higher up the stalk as the leaves become lighter, until you reach the center.

LEEKS COLLECT SOIL between their layers because of how they're grown, so thorough washing is essential. If you're slicing, dicing, or julienning leeks, it's easier and more effective to clean them *after* they're cut. Just immerse the pieces in a bowl of cold water, swishing them vigorously. Let them sit for a minute so the grit settles, and then gently scoop them out.

how and when to wash leeks

dicing

Cutting a leek into a fine dice is similar to dicing an onion: The root end stays attached (trim the hairy ends, if you want), but there's no need for horizontal slices.

the top. (For slender leeks, don't bother halving it; just make several lengthwise cuts all the way around the leek at the intervals you desire.) You should have many thin strands all held together at the root.

1 If the leek is thick, halve it lengthwise through the root. Make several lengthwise cuts at the width you need, from the root to

2 Bunch together the strands in a neat, tight bundle, and cut them crosswise into dice.

carrots, zucchini, cucumbers, and other cylindrical vegetables

ONCE THEY'RE PEELED AND TRIMMED, most cylindrical vegetables can be cut in a similar way. Trimming sometimes complicates matters—for example, thicker parsnips must be quartered lengthwise so the tough core can be cut away—but for the most part, one long, narrow vegetable is very much like another when it comes to slicing and dicing.

slicing

Not much to it. Just cut across the vegetable for rounds (or turn the knife on a diagonal for oblong slices). If you don't mind imperfect circles, shave a very thin slice off the side of the vegetable and set it on that flat side before slicing. This stabilizes the vegetable while cutting.

roll cut

Sometimes called an oblique cut, this is an uncommon way to cut long, narrow vegetables like carrots or asparagus. You end up with jaunty chunks with lots of angles and flat surfaces—a nice change of pace from the usual dice. When roll-cutting carrots,

you'll get more evenly sized pieces if you use slender roots that don't taper too dramatically from stem to tip.

1 Angle the knife and make a diagonal cut across the carrot to cut off one end. Hold the knife in the same position, roll the carrot 180 degrees, and cut again across the carrot, using the same diagonal slice. You'll end up with a carrot chunk with two converging flat sides.

2 Roll the carrot 180 degrees again, keeping the knife in the same diagonal position, and cut again. Continue cutting pieces, holding the knife in a diagonal position throughout.

julienning and dicing

This produces a ¼-inch julienne and dice; adjust the width of the cuts for larger or smaller dice. Whatever width you use, try to be consistent throughout for uniform pieces. Be aware that if the vegetable is quite slender, or if your goal is a larger dice, you'll only need to make one or two lengthwise cuts in steps 2 and 3.

1   Cut the vegetable crosswise into manageable (2- or 3-inch) lengths. Cut a ¼-inch-thick slice off one side. Set the vegetable on the flat side.

2   Slice the vegetable lengthwise into ¼-inch-thick planks. When it gets too wobbly to slice easily, you can turn it onto its wider flat side, if you want.

3   Stack two or three planks and cut them lengthwise into ¼-inch-thick strips (or julienne).

4   Gather several strips together neatly, and cut across them at ¼-inch intervals.

zucchini, corn, and red pepper sauté

This fresh, vibrant summer vegetable dish gives your knife skills an all-around workout. It's important to prep all the ingredients at the start because once you start cooking, everything goes quickly. Serve warm or at room temperature with roast chicken or grilled salmon.

SERVES 4 TO 6 AS A SIDE DISH

1 small leek

2 red bell peppers

1 (1 x 1½-inch) knob ginger

1 clove garlic

2 small zucchini

3 ears fresh corn

¼ cup extra-virgin olive oil

1 teaspoon kosher salt

¼ cup finely chopped fresh herbs (such as cilantro, parsley, or mint, or a combination; see page 132)

3 ounces feta cheese, crumbled (optional)

2 to 3 teaspoons fresh lemon juice

Freshly ground black pepper

CUT all the vegetables and place in individual bowls: Trim the leek and cut the white and light green parts into ¼-inch dice (see page 107). Core the peppers and cut into ⅜-inch dice (see page 116). Peel the ginger and mince it to yield about 1 tablespoon (see page 104). Finely chop the garlic (see page 100). Trim the ends of the zucchini and cut them into ¼-inch dice (see page 109). Shuck the corn and cut the kernels off the cob.

HEAT 3 tablespoons of the oil in a large (12-inch) skillet over medium heat. Add the leek and peppers and sprinkle with ¼ teaspoon of the salt. Cook, stirring often, until the vegetables are softened but not browned, about 3 minutes.

PUSH the vegetables to the perimeter of the pan and pour the remaining 1 tablespoon olive oil into the center. Add the ginger and garlic, and cook, stirring constantly, for about 30 seconds. Increase the heat to medium-high, add the zucchini, season with ½ teaspoon of the salt, and cook, stirring all the vegetables together, until the zucchini is just barely tender, 3 to 5 minutes.

ADD the corn, season with the remaining ¼ teaspoon salt, and cook, stirring often, until the corn is hot and the zucchini is tender (it shouldn't be mushy), about 2 minutes. Remove from the heat and let rest a few minutes.

SPRINKLE with the herbs and the feta, and toss gently. Add the lemon juice, and season with salt and pepper to taste.

spanish potato tortilla with serrano ham

Don't let the name confuse you. This is a hearty omelet, a mainstay in tapas bars throughout Spain. Serrano ham is the Iberian equivalent of Italian prosciutto; ask for it in specialty stores, or you can omit it entirely. If you own a ceramic santoku knife, use it to slice the potatoes; its smooth surface minimizes sticking.

SERVES 10 TO 12 AS AN APPETIZER, 4 TO 6 AS A LIGHT MAIN COURSE

1¾ cups corn oil, plus 1 tablespoon

5 Yukon Gold or white potatoes (1¾ pounds total), peeled and cut into ⅛-inch thick slices (see page 112)

2¼ teaspoons kosher salt

2 large yellow onions (about 12 ounces total), cut into ½-inch dice (see page 96)

6 large eggs

2 or 3 slices thinly sliced serrano ham or prosciutto, cut into ½-inch pieces

HEAT the 1¾ cups oil in a 10-inch non-stick skillet over medium-high heat. Put the potatoes in a bowl and sprinkle with 2 teaspoons of the salt. Toss to distribute. Test the temperature of the oil: If a slice of potato sizzles vigorously without browning, it is hot enough. Gently slide the potatoes into the oil, using a slotted metal spatula or skimmer. Cook them, turning occasionally, until tender but not browned, 10 to 12 minutes; you may need to lower the heat. Set a large sieve or colander over a bowl. Using the slotted spatula or skimmer, transfer the potatoes to the sieve to drain.

ADD the onions to the pan. Cook, adjusting the heat as needed, until very soft and translucent but not browned, 9 to 11 minutes. Remove from the heat and transfer the onions to the sieve. Pour out the oil from the skillet (save or discard). Wipe out the pan with a paper towel.

IN a large bowl, beat the eggs with the remaining ¼ teaspoon salt just until blended.

Add the potatoes, onions, and ham, and mix gently to combine with the egg. Try not to break the potatoes too much.

SET the skillet on medium-high heat (if the pan isn't nonstick, give it a minute or two to get good and hot). Add the remaining 1 tablespoon oil to the pan. When the oil is shimmering, pour in the potato mixture, spreading it evenly. Cook just enough to set the eggs on the sides and bottom of the pan, 30 seconds to 1 minute, and then immediately lower the heat to medium-low. Cook until the eggs are set near the edge but a little loose in the center, 8 to 10 minutes; the tortilla should slip around in the pan when you give it a shake.

TO flip the tortilla, set a 10-inch or larger flat plate upside-down over the pan. Lift the skillet off the burner and, with one hand pressing the plate securely against the skillet and the other hand holding the pan, invert the skillet so the tortilla lands on the plate (in one piece, ideally). Set the pan down and slide the tortilla into it while using the spatula to nudge any filling back under the eggs. Once the tortilla is in the pan, use the spatula to tuck the edges in to neaten the sides.

COOK over medium-low heat until the tortilla is firm in the center, 5 to 6 minutes more; a skewer inserted into the center should come out clean and hot. Transfer to a serving platter and let cool for at least 10 minutes. Serve warm, at room temperature, or cold, cutting it into wedges or small squares.

potatoes, beets, and other spherical vegetables

LIKE CYLINDRICALS, most roundish, dense vegetables can be cut in much the same way once they're peeled and trimmed. This category includes many of the underappreciated root vegetables, such as turnips and celery root, as well as sweet potatoes and even eggplants, which aren't usually spherical (though some varieties are) but whose bulbous shapes can be handled as though they were.

slicing, julienning, and dicing

1 Cut a slice off one side of the vegetable. Set the vegetable on the flat side. Slice the vegetable as thick or thin as needed.

2 Stack 2 or 3 slices of vegetable. (If making large dice, it may be unwieldy to stack; just line them up.) Cut them into strips whose width matches the width of the slices. This is your julienne.

3 To continue on to dice, gather a few strips together. Cut across them at the same width as before to produce even cubes.

cutting wedges

Cutting through the rounded side is safer, and it also gives you more control over the size of the wedge. This approach to wedges not only works well for potatoes, beets, and other round vegetables, but also for fennel, carrots, oranges, and many other ingredients.

1 Trim the vegetable as needed. Cut it in half; if it's truly spherical, it won't matter which way you cut (if it is more obloid than spherical, halve it lengthwise).

2 Set both halves flat side down. Cut one of the halves in half again (lengthwise if possible) so you have 2 quarters.

3 Keeping the 2 quarters together, cut them both in half (or thirds or quarters, if you want thinner wedges).

tip WHENEVER POSSIBLE, set the vegetable or fruit on a flat side so it doesn't wobble as you cut. If there is no flat side, create one by cutting a thin slice off one end.

roasted beet salad with goat cheese and toasted walnuts

If you think you don't like beets, it can only mean you've never tried roasting them—they become addictively sweet and tender. There's no need to peel them; the skin becomes quite tender during roasting. After making this salad, you'll be proficient at cutting even wedges.

SERVES 4 AS A FIRST COURSE

2 or 3 medium beets (1 pound total)

3 tablespoons extra-virgin olive oil

Kosher salt

½ cup walnut halves

1 tablespoon walnut oil

1 tablespoon sherry vinegar

1 teaspoon fresh thyme leaves, lightly chopped

Freshly ground black pepper

5 lightly packed cups (8 ounces) mixed baby greens, washed and spun dry

1 small package (3½ or 4 ounces) fresh goat cheese, cut into chunks

PREHEAT the oven to 400°F.

TRIM off the root and stem from the beets. Cut the beets into ½-inch wedges (see page 113). Put them in a bowl and toss with 1 tablespoon of the olive oil and a pinch of salt. On a baking sheet, arrange the beets with one flat side down. Roast until the bottom side is bubbly and starting to crisp, about 20 minutes. Turn each wedge and continue roasting until the beets are tender, about 7 more minutes. Remove from the oven and set aside.

SPREAD the walnuts on a small rimmed baking sheet. Toast in the oven (with the beets, if you want) until the nuts are aromatic, about 10 minutes. Transfer the nuts to a plate to cool.

WHISK the remaining 2 tablespoons olive oil, the walnut oil, vinegar, and thyme together in a small bowl. Whisk in salt and pepper to taste.

TOSS the greens in a large bowl with just enough of the vinaigrette to very lightly coat them—you'll need about three-quarters of the vinaigrette. Pile one-quarter of the greens on each plate. Distribute the beets, goat cheese, and walnuts around and on top of the greens. Drizzle with a little of the remaining vinaigrette.

bell peppers

julienning and dicing

This method removes the entire seed core intact, giving you an empty shell to cut into neat dice. It works best with blocky peppers with a broad, square base rather than narrower ones with pointed tips.

1 Cut off the top of the pepper to remove the shoulders. Cut off a slice from the bottom. (Dice these trimmings separately, or save them for vegetable stock.)

2 Cut into the side of the pepper to break into the interior.

3 Turn the knife so the blade is horizontal, and cut through the ribs as you roll away the seed core in one piece.

4 Cut the empty pepper shell crosswise into two pieces. If necessary, trim away any remaining white pith. Press on one piece to flatten it and cut strips at the width you need. This is your julienne.

5 Turn the slices and cut across them to create a dice.

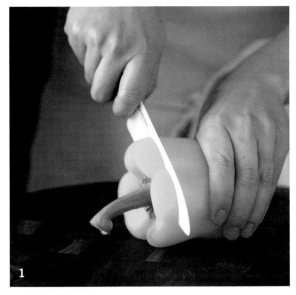

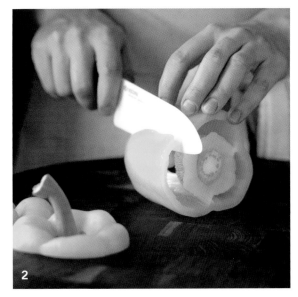

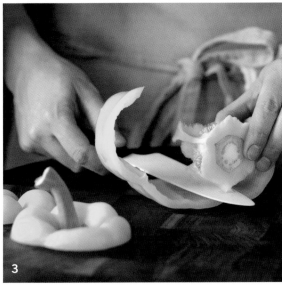

broccoli

cutting florets

1 Pull off any small leaves from the stem and florets. Cut off the tough bottom portion of the stem, usually about 2 inches. If you're not sure how much of the stalk to trim, start cutting close to the end and work your way up; you've reached the tender section when the knife meets less resistance. Discard the leaves and trimmings.

2 Cut off the stem at the point where most of the florets begin to branch off; reserve the stem.

3 Cut through the base of the floret stems to separate them. If you need smaller florets, cut through the stems again. Avoid cutting through the buds if possible, so as not to produce excess broccoli crumbs.

handling the stem

1 Cut off any protruding stubs on the stem to smooth it out. Peel the outer layer of stem with a sharp vegetable peeler or paring knife, to expose the tender flesh.

2 Cut the stem into slices, julienne, or dice as desired.

fennel

trimming, coring, slicing, and dicing

If you're braising or roasting fennel wedges, leave the core intact so it holds the fennel together. But for slicing or dicing, do cut away the core first. Lengthwise slices emphasize the vegetable's tough and fibrous quality. Crosswise slices are more tender and juicy, and better for salads.

1 Cut off the stalks close to the bulb (save the fernlike fronds for a garnish, if you want). Trim off the hard base. If the outer layer isn't too blemished or fibrous, leave it on. Otherwise, remove it and discard (or save for stock).

2 Cut the bulb into lengthwise quarters. Stand up one quarter on its base, or let it rest on the rounded side, and cut away the core. Repeat with the other three pieces.

3 Set the pieces on a flat side. Cut crosswise or lengthwise slices of the width you need. (For a dice, cut lengthwise slices and gather a few strips and cut across them.)

spicy steamed mussels with fennel and tomatoes

This punchy rendition of mussels in white wine offers a quick course on several cuts: slicing, dicing, mincing, and chiffonading. Serve the mussels with crusty bread for dipping into the peppery tomato broth, or ladle the mussels and broth over hot linguine. When buying mussels, ask the fishmonger for a bag from the refrigerator in back, which are often fresher than those in the front display.

SERVES 2 TO 3 AS A MAIN COURSE

1 small fennel bulb

1 small yellow onion

1 carrot

3 cloves garlic

2 small tomatoes

10 to 12 large fresh basil leaves

1 teaspoon black peppercorns

½ teaspoon fennel seeds

½ teaspoon kosher salt

⅛ teaspoon red pepper flakes

3 tablespoons extra-virgin olive oil

¾ cup dry white wine

2 pounds mussels, scrubbed and debearded (discard any that do not close)

TRIM the stalks from the fennel and cut a thin slice off the bottom; then core and cut the fennel into ¼-inch crosswise slices (see page 119). Put the fennel into a large bowl. Cut the onion crosswise into ¼-inch semi-circles (see page 95) and add to the bowl. Peel the carrot and cut into ¼-inch dice (see page 109) and add to the bowl. Peel and mince the garlic (see page 100) and add to the bowl.

CORE the tomatoes. Cut them in half through the equator and squeeze out the seeds. Cut them into ¼-inch dice (see page 127) and put them in a separate bowl. Cut the basil into chiffonade (see page 133) and reserve for the garnish.

LIGHTLY crush the peppercorns and fennel seeds in a mortar and pestle. (Alternatively, put them in a small self-sealing plastic bag. Using the bottom of a cast-iron skillet, lightly crush them. Transfer the spices to a small dish.) Add the salt and red pepper flakes. Set aside.

HEAT the oil in a heavy 6-quart or larger stockpot over medium heat. Add the fennel, onion, carrot, and garlic, and sauté, stirring occasionally, until softened but not browned, about 5 minutes. Stir in the spice mixture. Add the wine and the tomatoes along with any juices in the bowl. Bring to a boil.

ADD the mussels to the stockpot (don't stir), cover, and steam until the mussels open, about 5 minutes. Scoop the mussels into individual shallow bowls, discarding any that remain closed, and then spoon some vegetables and broth over them. Sprinkle each bowl with basil and serve immediately.

artichokes

trimming to the heart

Getting to the meaty bottom of an artichoke produces a fair amount of waste, but it's a necessary evil if you want to use the vegetable in risotto, omelets, or a simple sauté. To prevent the artichokes from turning brown once they're cut, rub each cut side with a lemon half as you trim. Deposit the trimmed pieces in a bowl of acidulated water (add about a teaspoon or so of lemon juice) until you're ready to cook them. Also, don't use a carbon steel knife on artichokes because it will cause the flesh to darken.

1 Cut off most of the stem. (Trim off the dried end, and peel and cut up the stem, if you want, or else discard it.) Snap off the first few layers of dark green outer leaves. Continue removing leaves until you reach the tender, yellowish leaves toward the center.

2 Cut off the remaining leaves about an inch above the base (just above the leaves' natural indentation).

3 Using a paring knife, trim away the fibrous dark green layer around the base.

4 Cut the heart in half lengthwise (through the stem). Using a measuring spoon or melon baller, scoop out the hairy choke and any inner leaves that remain. Drop the two halves into a bowl of acidulated water while you trim any remaining artichokes.

5 Before cooking, cut the hearts into wedges, slices, or dice as needed.

cauliflower

cutting florets

Some cooks prefer to keep cauliflower florets intact for a holistic look. To do this, divide the florets through the stem only and then break the tops apart by hand—they fracture along natural lines. The approach shown here produces more crumbs, but you end up with florets with flat surfaces, which caramelize better when roasting and sautéing.

1 Cut or pull off the large stiff leaves around the head. Trim off the stem as close to the florets as possible.

2 Set the head on the flat stem end and cut through the top to halve it.

3 Cut the large florets off the core.

4 Slice straight through the large florets to break them down into smaller sizes as needed.

roasted cauliflower-gruyère gratin

Here's a scrumptious way to get your fill of cauliflower and practice cutting florets. Commercially packaged bread crumbs are too powdery for this dish; make your own in a food processor or request them from your local bread bakery.

SERVES 4 TO 6 AS A SIDE DISH

1 medium head cauliflower

5 tablespoons extra-virgin olive oil

¾ teaspoon kosher salt

1 cup fresh coarse bread crumbs

1 cup (3 ounces) grated Gruyère cheese

Pinch of nutmeg, preferably freshly grated

Freshly ground black pepper

¾ cup heavy cream

PREHEAT the oven to 450°F.

TRIM the cauliflower and cut it into florets that are 1½ inches wide at their widest point (see opposite page). Put the florets on a small baking sheet, drizzle with 3 tablespoons of the oil, and sprinkle with ½ teaspoon of the salt. Toss to coat. Arrange the florets cut side down. Roast until the florets are just barely tender and golden brown on the bottom, 20 to 25 minutes. Remove from the oven and keep the oven on.

COMBINE the bread crumbs, the remaining 2 tablespoons oil, and the remaining ¼ teaspoon salt in a medium bowl. Stir well. Add the cheese and stir to combine.

DISTRIBUTE the cauliflower evenly in an 8-cup baking dish (7 by 11-inch works well). Sprinkle the nutmeg over the florets, along with a few grindings of pepper. Top with the cream. Distribute the bread crumb mixture evenly on top. Bake until the topping is golden and crispy and the cream has thickened a little, 15 to 20 minutes. Remove from the oven and let rest about 10 minutes before serving. Serve warm or at room temperature.

tomatoes

AS ALMOST EVERYONE KNOWS, the key to happy tomato cutting is a super-sharp knife. If you don't have one, the next best thing is a tomato knife (page 37) or any knife with a serrated edge.

coring and slicing

Latitudinal slices (parallel to the tomato's "equator") constrain the seeds better and are prettier for burgers and sandwiches.

1   Core the tomato: choke up on a short paring knife and insert the tip into the stem. Rotate the tomato as you push the blade around the stem.

2   Starting on either the stem or blossom end, cut horizontal slices at the width you need.

tip WHEN YOU WANT the fleshy meat but not the seeds of a tomato, core it and then cut it in half through the equator. Squeeze each half gently over a dish or sink to discharge the pulp and seeds. You may need to nudge out the last bits with a small spoon or your fingertip. Now you can dice the flesh as needed.

dicing

This is similar to the grid method of dicing an onion, except you're cutting all the way through the tomato instead of leaving one end attached.

1 Halve the tomato lengthwise through the stem, and notch out the core from both halves.

2 Make horizontal cuts at the desired width, cutting all the way through the tomato. Cut vertical slices at the same even intervals to get strips.

3 Cut across the strips for an even dice.

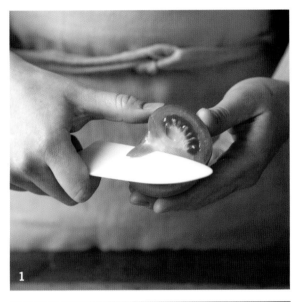

tomato, cucumber, and feta salad with avocado

This riff on Bulgarian *shopska,* which typically consists of tomato, cucumber, feta, and green onions, is all about dicing. The avocado makes this version deliciously unique: its buttery texture plays off the crunchy cucumber and juicy tomato. If you're feeling adventurous, try tossing in a handful of toasted pine nuts, too. When serving to guests, bring the salad to the table *before* you toss it, for a crisp and pretty presentation.

SERVES 4 TO 6 AS A FIRST COURSE

2 medium-large tomatoes

½ large seedless cucumber (6-inch piece)

4 green onions

1 cup (5 ounces) crumbled feta cheese

½ cup pitted kalamata olives, halved lengthwise

2½ tablespoons fresh lemon juice

2 tablespoons extra-virgin olive oil

1 firm but ripe Hass avocado

2 tablespoons medium-chopped fresh flat-leaf parsley (optional) (see page 132)

Good-quality bread, for serving

CUT the tomatoes into ½-inch dice and put them in a large bowl (see page 127). Cut the cucumber into ½-inch dice and add them to the bowl (see page 109). Cut the white and light green parts of the green onions into ¼-inch pieces and add them to the bowl. Add the feta and olives to the bowl.

POUR the lemon juice and olive oil over the vegetables. Toss gently.

PIT the avocado and cut the flesh into ½-inch dice (see pages 136 and 137).

DISTRIBUTE the avocado on the salad, along with the parsley. Fold together very gently, just enough to distribute the avocado. Serve with bread to soak up the dressing that collects in the bottom of the bowl.

hardy greens

stemming and chopping

The thick, tough stems of Swiss chard, kale, and collard greens continue up into the leaf, so to trim the entire stem, you need to work with each leaf individually. Sometimes you can fold the leaf in half lengthwise (with the stem as the crease) and cut right along the side of the stem, removing it in one stroke. But if the leaf doesn't fold neatly, use the method shown here. Discard the stems—unless it's chard, whose stems may be chopped and cooked, if you want.

1 Set the leaf on the board so the front of the leaf faces down (ribs facing up). Cut along one side of the stem, and then along the other side. Then nip it across the top to separate it from the leaf.

2 To chop the leaves, stack a few on top of each other. If they're very broad, make a few lengthwise cuts. Then cut them crosswise into pieces.

tip **MANY COOKS USE their chef's knife to ferry diced vegetables from the board to a hot skillet or to gather herbs into a pile while chopping. That's fine, but be aware that scraping the blade across the board can degrade the edge. A better tool is a metal bench scraper; it's bigger and faster and its dull edge can take the abuse. Or you could flip your chef's knife over so you're scraping with the spine. But if you do use the cutting edge as a scraper—it is tempting, after all—just try to do it gently.**

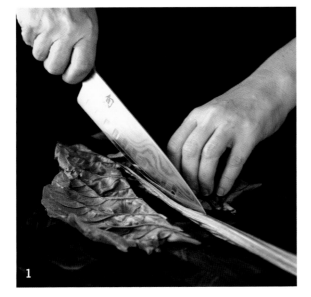

chard, mushroom, and swiss cheese frittata

The secret ingredient here is Dijon mustard. You won't taste it, but it's working behind the scenes to deepen the flavor. Chop the chard with your longest chef's knife for efficiency—a 10-incher is perfect.

SERVES 6

1 pound Swiss chard

¼ cup extra-virgin olive oil

8 ounces white mushrooms, thinly sliced

¾ teaspoon kosher salt, plus extra for sprinkling

¼ cup minced shallots (see page 97)

8 large eggs

¼ cup half-and-half

1 teaspoon Dijon mustard

Freshly ground black pepper

1⅔ cups (5 ounces) grated Gruyère or Jarlsburg cheese

PREHEAT the oven to 350°F.

TRIM the stems from the chard leaves (see page 129). Discard the stems. Immerse the leaves in water to rid them of grit. Lift them out and drain. Chop the leaves coarsely (see page 129).

HEAT 3 tablespoons of the oil in a 10-inch ovenproof skillet over medium-high heat. Add the mushrooms, sprinkle lightly with salt, and sauté, stirring frequently, until golden brown, 5 to 7 minutes. Lower the heat to medium, add the shallots, and cook until the shallots are softened but not browned, about 30 seconds. Add the chard a few handfuls at a time and cook, tossing with tongs, until soft and wilted, about 4 minutes. Add ¼ teaspoon of the salt and continue cooking and tossing until all the liquid in the pan evaporates, about 3 more minutes. Turn off the heat.

WHISK the eggs, half-and-half, mustard, the remaining ½ teaspoon salt, and several grinds of pepper together in a medium bowl. Stir in the cheese. Add the remaining 1 tablespoon olive oil to the skillet and heat over medium heat. Spread out the vegetables evenly and, when the pan is hot, pour in the egg mixture. Cook until the bottom is set, about 3 minutes, and then transfer the skillet to the oven. Bake until the eggs are set on top, about 15 minutes.

PLACE the frittata under the broiler a few inches from the heat source until the top is golden, 2 to 3 minutes. Remove from the heat and let rest for a few minutes; the frittata will pull away from the sides of the pan. Slice in the pan or else flip the frittata onto a plate and serve.

fresh herbs

chopping

For a fluffy pile of chopped herbs, start with a good sharp knife—a dull one bruises the leaves. Rinse the herbs in cool water and gently but thoroughly pat them dry with a paper towel (or use a salad spinner). Excess moisture makes the leaves sticky and flat. Use this chopping method for olives, capers, nuts, and other similarly small ingredients.

1 For a large bunch of parsley or cilantro, gather the stems in one hand and let the leaves rest on the board. Angle the blade so the side touches the stems, and "shave" off the leaves with short strokes, rotating the bunch with each cut. Pick out any thick stems that made it through. For hardy herbs such as rosemary and oregano and for small quantities of more tender herbs, pick off the leaves by hand. Discard the stems.

2 Gather the leaves in a tight mound. Rock the blade using an up-and-down stroke with a bit of forward motion (the locomotive) to coarsely chop the leaves.

3 After cutting through the pile once, gather the herbs into a pile again. Resting your fingertips on the tip of the knife, chop with a straight up-and-down motion, letting the knife arc from one side of the pile to the other. Scrape the herbs back into a pile and continue chopping in an arc until the herbs are as fine as you need.

cutting chiffonade

This creates thin strips of large-leafed herbs such as basil, mint, and sage.

1   Neatly stack several leaves, with the largest leaves on the bottom and all the tips facing the same direction.

2   Roll up the leaves lengthwise into a tight cigar.

3   Slice off thin strips from the roll, using your guiding hand to hold the roll together and being sure to cut all the way through to the board. Fluff the herbs with your fingers to separate the strands.

crispy roasted potato wedges with parsley, rosemary, and lemon

With a little chopping of herbs and garlic, you can step up your everyday roasted potatoes to something special. Lemon zest and parsley add sparkle, and the generous coating of olive oil helps ensure crispness.

SERVES 4 TO 6 AS A SIDE DISH

2 cloves garlic

½ cup extra-virgin olive oil

3 tablespoons finely chopped fresh flat-leaf parsley (see page 132)

2 teaspoons chopped fresh rosemary (see page 132)

2 pounds (7 or 8 small) unpeeled Yukon Gold, white, or red potatoes, scrubbed

1½ teaspoons kosher salt

Grated zest from 1 lemon (1 tablespoon lightly packed), plus the juice

PREHEAT the oven to 450°F. Finely chop the garlic (see page 100) and put it in a large bowl. Add the oil, parsley, and rosemary.

CUT the potatoes into ¾- to 1-inch-wide wedges (see page 113).

ADD the potatoes to the bowl and sprinkle with the salt. Toss with your hands to evenly coat the potatoes with the oil mixture.

SPREAD the potatoes on a large rimmed baking sheet, scraping the bowl of any extra oil and herbs, and arrange the potatoes with a flat side down. Roast until the bottom is golden, about 25 minutes, and then turn them with a metal spatula (some potatoes will stick, but do your best to scrape them loose). Continue roasting until golden and crisp outside and tender inside, about 15 minutes more. Gently sprinkle with the lemon zest.

TRANSFER the potatoes to a serving bowl, making sure to scrape up all the herbs and zest. Add several squeezes of the juice over the top. Toss gently to distribute. Serve hot.

avocados

halving and pitting

To pit an avocado safely, keep your hands out of the line of action. The usual advice is to hold the avocado in one hand, sling the blade into the pit, and then twist it out. That's risky business because the knife can slip off the pit and into your hand. (If you already use this method and plan to stick with it, at least take these precautions: Put a towel between your hand and the fruit, and carefully press the knife into the pit rather than wielding it like an axe.) Here is a safer way.

1   Set the avocado on the board and run the knife lengthwise around the center, from stem to blossom end, rotating the avocado as you cut. The knife should touch the pit.

2   Gently twist the two halves apart.

3   Nudge the pit with a soup spoon to pop it out. (Sometimes it releases quite easily, sometimes less so; just wiggle it free the best you can.)

scooping out the flesh

If the avocado isn't too ripe, you can sometimes peel away the skin with your hands. But if the flesh is a little soft, it's easier to use a spoon. Use this method when you need to slice or finely dice the fruit.

Slide a large metal spoon between the skin and flesh and carefully work the spoon underneath the flesh. Then slice, dice, or mash as needed.

dicing in the skin

Use this efficient technique when you need large dice.

1   To dice the avocado before it's been peeled, set the avocado half on the counter and score the flesh with the tip of a paring knife.

2   Slide a large metal spoon under the flesh to scoop it out.

chunky guacamole

This sassy recipe puts your avocado-pitting skills to the test, and adds a bit of mincing and dicing practice for good measure. Be sure to use pebbly-skinned Hass avocados rather than a larger smooth-skinned variety, which can be watery. The avocados must be ripe: They should give slightly when you press the skin.

MAKES ABOUT 2 CUPS

2 ripe Hass avocados

1 small tomato

½ very small red onion

3 tablespoons fresh lime juice

2 teaspoons minced jalapeño (seeded, if you want less heat), or more to taste

¼ teaspoon kosher salt

Pinch of ground cumin

CUT the avocados in half and remove the pit (see page 136). Scoop the avocado flesh into a bowl. Mash with a fork to a chunky consistency.

CORE the tomato, cut it in half through the equator and squeeze out the seeds, and cut into ¼-inch dice (see page 127). You should have about ½ cup. Mince the onion (see page 96); you should have 3 tablespoons (discard any extra). Add the tomato, onion, lime juice, jalapeño, salt, and cumin to the avocado. Stir to blend. Taste and adjust the seasoning of the salt, lime, and jalapeño. Cover with plastic wrap directly on the guacamole, and refrigerate for 15 to 30 minutes to let the flavors develop.

apples

CUTTING UP APPLES FOR PIES, tarts, and other desserts isn't difficult, but it can be tedious. Here's a method that cuts the juicy flesh off the core in just four straight cuts—no need to fuss with a corer or to carve out the seeds with a paring knife.

slicing and dicing

1 Peel the apple if needed. Set the knife about ⅓ inch or so away from the stem and cut off one side of the apple; you're aiming for the end of the seed core. Cut off the opposite side.

2 Set the apple on a flat side and cut off the remaining two sides. Discard the seed core.

3 Set the four pieces flat side down and slice or dice as needed.

flaky apple pinwheels

Simple and lovely on their own, these individual pastries are even better with a scoop of vanilla ice cream alongside or a dollop of crème fraîche. They're best when warm from the oven, so if it helps with timing, you can assemble them ahead and refrigerate for a couple of hours before baking (don't brush with egg until the last minute, though). Slicing the apples is a breeze; try to aim for uniform thickness so they cook evenly.

SERVES 4

2 medium apples (12 ounces), such as Braeburn, Gala, or Rome

¼ cup sugar

¼ teaspoon ground cinnamon

Scant ⅛ teaspoon nutmeg, preferably freshly ground

Pinch of kosher salt

1 sheet frozen puff pastry (9 ounces), thawed at room temperature for 45 minutes (keep refrigerated until ready to use)

1 tablespoon unsalted butter, cut into small pieces

1 large egg

Turbinado sugar, or another coarse sugar, for sprinkling (optional)

PREHEAT the oven to 400°F. Line a baking sheet with parchment paper. Peel the apples and cut them into ¼-inch-thick slices (see page 139). Put the apples in a medium bowl. Sprinkle with the sugar, cinnamon, nutmeg, and salt, and toss until evenly coated.

ON a lightly floured surface, gently unfold the puff pastry and roll it out to a 12-inch square (use a ruler; don't guesstimate). Cut it into four 6-inch squares. Put the squares on the lined baking sheet.

POUR a little water in a small dish. Set a mound of apples in the center of each pastry square, distributing them evenly. Drop the butter pieces evenly over the apples. Moisten the four corners of one of the pastry squares with the water. Lift up and join the corners together in the center, first squeezing them firmly and then giving a good hard twist (don't be shy; firm pressure is essential or the pinwheels may open during baking). Repeat with the other three squares.

LIGHTLY beat the egg in a small dish. Brush the pastries with the egg; be sure to coat all surfaces, including the sides and the center knob. Sprinkle each pastry with a little turbinado sugar. Bake until the pinwheels are deep golden on top and bottom (lift one up to check), about 25 minutes. Set the pan on a rack for 5 to 10 minutes before serving.

pineapples

THIS TROPICAL FRUIT MAY LOOK FORBIDDING, but don't be put off: its prickly skin yields easily to a sharp knife.

peeling

Cut off the spiky top of the pineapple and a thin slice off the bottom. Stand the pineapple up and cut down the side, aiming to remove most of the eyes and not too much excess flesh. Rotate the pineapple and cut again to remove the skin. Switch to a paring knife to shave any remaining tough eyes.

slicing rings

1 Trim the peeled pineapple with a chef's knife to round off any sharp corners (this will ensure more perfect circles). Set the pineapple on its side and cut slices.

2 Use a 1½-inch biscuit cutter (or paring knife) to stamp out the core from each piece.

cutting wedges

1 Stand up the peeled pineapple and cut it lengthwise into quarters. Stand up one quarter and cut out the tough core.

2 Set the quarters on a flat side and cut wedges of the size you need.

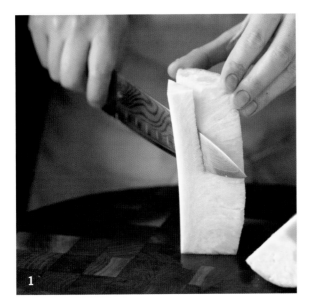

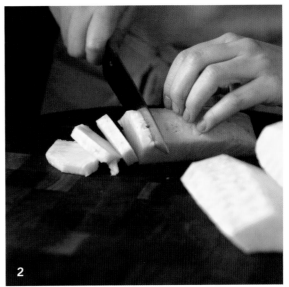

mangoes

FOR SUCH A SUCCULENT FRUIT, mangoes sure are a pain to peel and pit. Here are two options.

method 1: dice first, then peel

The advantage to this approach is that you don't have to grip the slippery flesh. It works best when you need ½-inch dice or larger.

1   Cut a thin slice off the stem end of the mango to create a flat base. With the knife a little off the center point, slice off one broad cheek of the mango. The knife should barely rub against the pit on its way down. Cut the other cheek off the same way.

2   Score the flesh with the tip of a paring knife in a crosshatch pattern, creating the size dice you want. Be careful not to cut through the skin.

3   Invert the mango half so the cubes pop out. Cut the cubes away from the skin. Repeat with the other half. Cut the two thinner sides off of the pit and handle them the same way.

method 2: peel first, then slice or dice

1 Cut a thin slice off the stem end of the mango to create a flat base. Stand up the mango and cut away the skin, following the gentle curve of the fruit.

2 With the knife a little off the center point, slice off one broad cheek of the mango. The knife should barely rub against the pit on its way down. Cut the other cheek off the same way.

3 Cut off the two narrower sides, following the curve of the pit. There is minimal flesh on these sides.

4 Slice or dice the mango as needed.

mango-cucumber salsa

There's lots of dicing and mincing to do here, but once that's out of the way, you just toss everything together and you're done. This makes a fresh, colorful condiment for grilled or sautéed pork chops, chicken breasts, or fish fillets.

MAKES ABOUT 2 CUPS

2 small, ripe mangoes

½ seedless cucumber (about 6 inches), peeled

¼ red bell pepper

2 tablespoons minced fresh cilantro (see page 132), plus a stem for garnish

1 green onion, white and light green parts only, sliced thinly

1 jalapeño, seeded and minced

1 tablespoon fresh lime juice, plus more as needed

Pinch of sugar

Kosher salt and freshly ground black pepper

PEEL and pit the mango and cut the flesh into ¼-inch dice (see pages 144 and 145). Cut the cucumber into ¼-inch dice (see page 109). Cut the bell pepper into ¼-inch dice (see page 116).

PUT the mangoes, cucumber, bell pepper, cilantro, green onion, and jalapeño in a medium bowl. Toss to combine. Add the lime juice, sugar, and salt and pepper to taste. Toss, taste, and adjust the seasoning. Garnish with cilantro stem if desired. Serve immediately, or refrigerate for up to 12 hours.

fennel and orange salad with fresh cranberries and green apple

Bright, tangy, and full of fall flavors, this slawlike salad will jazz up a pork, chicken, or turkey main course. It also lets you hone your fennel slicing and orange-segmenting skills. Reducing the orange juice is the key to the dressing's intense flavor.

SERVES 4 AS A SIDE DISH

⅔ cup fresh cranberries

2 tablespoons sugar

3 navel or blood oranges (or a mix)

1 fennel bulb

¼ small red onion

1 small Granny Smith apple

2 tablespoons coarsely chopped fresh flat-leaf parsley (see page 132)

1 tablespoon extra-virgin olive oil

1 tablespoon red wine vinegar

½ teaspoon kosher salt, plus a pinch

Freshly ground black pepper

SET a cutting board in a large rimmed baking sheet (to catch any runaway cranberries). Cut the berries in half, cupping your hand over the spine of the knife to help prevent berries from popping off the board. Continue chopping them to medium-coarse pieces, as for a relish. Put the cranberries in a small bowl and toss with the sugar. Let macerate for about 20 minutes as you prepare the rest of the ingredients.

WORKING over a bowl, segment the oranges (see page 150). Pick out any stray seeds. Separate the orange segments from their juice, reserving both in separate bowls.

PEEL away the outer layer of fennel if it is scuffed up or very fibrous. Quarter and core the fennel, and cut it into very thin crosswise slices (see page 119); you should have 2 to 2½ cups. Put the fennel in a large bowl. Cut the onion into very thin crosswise slices until you get ¼ cup (see page 94), and add it to the bowl.

PEEL the apple and cut it into ⅜-inch-thick slices (see page 139). Cut the slices into ⅜-inch julienne strips and then crosswise into ⅜-inch dice; you should have 1 cup. Add the apple to the bowl with the fennel. Add the parsley to the bowl as well.

COMBINE the olive oil, vinegar, and a generous pinch of salt in a small dish. Pour the reserved orange juice into a very small saucepan. Give the orange segments a gentle squeeze to release additional juice and add the juices to the pan. Bring the juice to a simmer and let it reduce down to a thin, syrupy consistency, 2 to 3 minutes; you should have about 1 tablespoon of juice. Add it to the oil mixture.

SPRINKLE the fennel mixture with the ½ teaspoon salt and a few grinds of pepper. Scrape the cranberries, along with any juices, into the bowl. Add the orange segments (but not their juices, if any) and toss gently. Whisk the dressing and drizzle it over the salad. Toss to coat. Refrigerate for at least 30 minutes or up to 12 hours. Taste and add salt if needed before serving.

oranges and other citrus fruit

segmenting

Orange segments, also called supremes, let you enjoy the sweet flesh without the pithy membranes. In salads, they make a more elegant presentation. You can use this technique for grapefruit too.

1 Using a paring knife, cut off the top and bottom of the orange to expose the flesh. Set the orange on a cut side and, following the curve of the fruit, cut off the skin in strips. Try to remove all the white pith but not too much of the flesh. Trim off any missed bits of pith.

2 Holding the orange over a bowl, cut alongside the membrane on each side of the segment until it releases and falls into the bowl. Rotate the orange and free the next segment the same way. When you have freed all the segments, squeeze the membrane to release its juices into the bowl.

chocolate

shaving a thick block

Use a chef's knife or a stiff serrated bread knife to chop a thick block of chocolate into small chips for baking or melting. Avoid using the tip of a chef's knife to break the block apart. The tip could snap or slip.

1 Set the heel of the chef's knife or the middle portion of a serrated knife near the edge of one corner of the chocolate.

2 Apply pressure to the spine of the knife as you shave off thin or thick shards. (If the pieces are too large, cut across them, keeping your hand on the tip of the knife, letting the blade pivot in an arc from the tip, as for chopping herbs or mincing garlic.)

CHOPPED CHOCOLATE AND COCOA POWDER create a rich, intense chocolate flavor in this glossy sauce. Store in the refrigerator for up to ten days; reheat gently over medium heat or in the microwave. Makes 1 cup.

decadent hot fudge sauce

Combine ½ cup heavy cream, 3 tablespoons light corn syrup, 1 tablespoon Dutch-processed cocoa powder, and a pinch of salt in a small saucepan. Bring to a simmer over medium-high heat, whisking to dissolve the cocoa powder. Remove the pan from the heat. Add 4 ounces of bittersweet chocolate, chopped medium fine (see above) and whisk until melted. Whisk in ¼ teaspoon vanilla. Serve immediately or let cool slightly for a thicker consistency.

BUTCHERING RAW MEAT or poultry and filleting fish definitely puts you into advanced knife-skills territory. The stakes are higher, too, because meat and fish are more costly than produce, and mistakes are hard to hide. But don't let that stop you from giving it a try if you're so inclined. The good news is that carving cooked meats isn't as tricky, especially when you have the right tool (a thin, sharp knife) and a plan for how to do it (which you'll find here).

poultry, meat, and fish

cutting a chicken into parts

CUTTING UP A CHICKEN YOURSELF is more economical than buying prepackaged parts, and it's relatively simple, plus you get the back and wings for stock. This method gives you eight fairly even-sized pieces, ready for braising, roasting, frying, or grilling. You can do the whole operation with a chef's knife (preferably a hefty German-style since you'll be cutting through bone), but it's helpful to have a paring knife and meat cleaver on deck too.

1 Set the bird with the back facing up and the wings nearest you. Extend one wing and cut through the skin at the joint closest to the back. Remove the entire wing by cutting through the joint, angling the knife edge toward the wing to avoid removing any breast meat. Spin the chicken around and remove the other wing. Save the wings for stock.

2 Turn the bird over so the breast faces up and the legs are nearest you. Extend one leg and cut through the skin—you shouldn't be cutting through meat yet—so the leg pulls away from the body.

3 As you get close to the back, it is helpful to switch to a paring knife. Turn the bird on its side and feel for the "oyster," a meaty nugget tucked in a divot between the back and the thigh. Carefully scrape the tip of the knife under the oyster and along the bone to keep the oyster attached to the thigh.

  Turn the chicken back so the breast faces up. Bend back the leg to expose the joint. Using a chef's knife, cut through the joint and meat to separate the leg from the back. Remove the other leg the same way.

4 Separate the thigh and drumstick by cutting through the thin line of fat on the underside of the leg. The joint is usually just under this line, or else a smidgen closer to the drumstick. Repeat with the other leg. Trim any excess fat and skin.

5 Remove the back by cutting through the wispy sheet of muscle connecting the breast to the backbone. Switch to a meat cleaver or shears, if you want, to continue cutting through the ribs. Bend the back away from the breast. Chop through the bones on either side of the neck to separate the back. Save the back for stock.

6 Set the breast on the board, skin side down. Set a cleaver or chef's knife in the center of the breastbone and press down very hard to cleave the breast in half. Trim the breasts of any excess skin or fat.

7 Turn the breasts skin side up and use a cleaver or chef's knife to cut each breast into two fairly even pieces, angling the cut to avoid splintering the vertical keel bone.

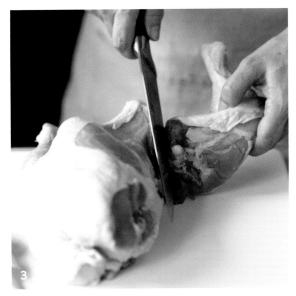

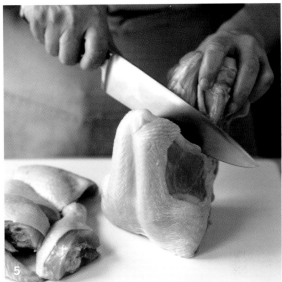

arroz con pollo with chorizo and capers

When using a cut-up whole chicken (rather than only legs and thighs) for this dish, you need to take precautions to keep the breast meat from drying out. The trick is to sear the breast pieces briefly and then add them to the rice halfway through cooking. Mexican chorizo, a fresh sausage seasoned with garlic and paprika, delivers more authentic flavor. Look for it in Hispanic groceries.

SERVES 6 AS A MAIN COURSE

8 ounces Mexican chorizo or sweet Italian sausage

1 (3- to 3½-pound) chicken, cut into 8 serving pieces (see page 154), wings and back reserved for stock

2½ teaspoons kosher salt

Freshly ground black pepper

3 tablespoons extra-virgin olive oil

1½ teaspoons ground cumin

¾ teaspoon paprika

¼ teaspoon ground turmeric

⅛ teaspoon chili powder

1 onion, cut into ¼-inch dice (see page 96)

1 red bell pepper, cut into ½-inch dice (see page 116)

5 large cloves garlic, chopped coarsely (see page 100)

¾ cup dry white wine

¾ cup crushed canned tomatoes

1 bay leaf

2¼ cups medium-grain rice

2½ cups chicken broth

3 tablespoons capers in brine, drained but not rinsed

Lemon wedges and hot sauce, for serving (optional)

CUT the chorizo in half lengthwise, then crosswise into 1-inch chunks (it's easier if the casing side is up; the casing shouldn't come off, but if it does, just discard it). Set aside.

PAT the chicken pieces dry with paper towels. Season with 2 teaspoons of the kosher salt and a few grinds of pepper. Heat the oil in a medium (5-quart) Dutch oven or heavy casserole over medium-high heat. Sear the drumsticks and thighs until deeply golden on all sides, 7 to 10 minutes (use a splatter screen if you have one). Transfer the pieces to a large bowl. Sear the breast pieces on the skin side only until golden, about 3 minutes. Transfer them to the bowl. Lower the heat to medium and sear the chorizo, stirring frequently, until golden brown, 2 to 3 minutes. Transfer the chorizo to the bowl.

POUR off and discard all but 1 tablespoon of oil. Spoon out any burnt bits. Combine the cumin, paprika, turmeric, and chili powder in a small dish. Set the pot over medium heat and add the onion and bell pepper. Cook for 2 minutes, stirring often; the moisture in the vegetables will deglaze the browned drippings in the pan. Add the garlic and cook, stirring, until the vegetables are softened, about 3 minutes. Add the measured spices and cook, stirring, for 1 minute to let the flavors bloom.

ADD the wine, tomatoes, the remaining ½ teaspoon salt, and the bay leaf. Increase the heat to medium-high and simmer for 2 minutes. Add the drumsticks, thighs, and chorizo to the pot. Add the rice and broth. Bring to a boil, cover, lower the heat to medium-low, and simmer for 9 minutes.

ADD the breast pieces to the pot, nestling them into the rice, and continue simmer-ing until the rice is tender and the liquid is absorbed, about 9 minutes more.

REMOVE the pan from the heat and let rest, covered, for 5 minutes. Sprinkle the capers on top of the rice. When spooning out portions, look for the bay leaf and discard it. Serve with the lemon wedges and hot sauce.

boning a chicken breast

ONE ADVANTAGE TO BONING OUT A BREAST YOURSELF is that you can keep the skin on, which you may sometimes want (boneless, skin-on chicken breasts aren't usually available in supermarkets). It's not hard to do—the idea is to ease the meat away from the carcass, following the line of the breastbone. The method shown here works best on a whole breast or even a whole bird (freeze the legs, back, and wings for another use); for a split bone-in breast, you'll need to make little adjustments but the approach is the same. A small, sharp boning knife is perfect, or you could use a paring knife.

1 Set the breast skin side up with the wing joints closest to you. Feel for the top of the keel bone. Make an incision between the bone and meat, hugging the bone, and make short, shallow cuts down to the breastplate.

2 Ease the meat away from the bone while making short, backward swipes with the knife, working toward the ribs and always keeping the knife angled toward the bone (to avoid cutting into the flesh). Run the knife along the outside arm of the wishbone to cut the meat away.

3 When you reach the bone that was attached to the wing, cut around it. Cut through the skin to separate the breast.

4 If you want, pull away the narrow strip of breast meat, called the tenderloin, or tender, and cook it separately. Sometimes, it will separate from the breast on its own. Trim any excess skin or fat from the breast. Remove the other breast the same way.

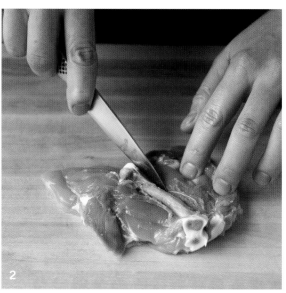

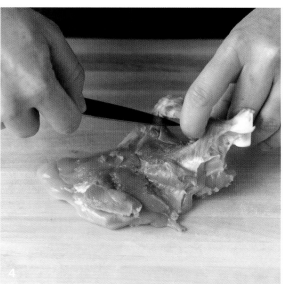

boning a chicken thigh

SOME SUPERMARKETS STOCK BONELESS CHICKEN THIGHS, but if they don't, just buy bone-in thighs. With a sharp paring knife, it takes about two minutes to remove the bone yourself.

1 Pull off the skin and cut off any large pieces of fat. Set the thigh so the side that had the skin faces down and the bonier side faces up. Make a straight cut right over the bone. Cut and scrape the meat away from one side of the bone, cutting around the joints as well.

2 Cut the meat away from the bone and joints on the other side the same way. The meat should lie flat, with the bone attached only on the underside.

3 Insert the tip of the knife underneath the bone and scrape away the meat to separate it.

4 Hook your finger under the bone and cut all the way around each joint to free the bone; work around the joints carefully to capture any smaller disjoined bone fragments. Feel the meat for any pieces of bone or cartilage that you may have missed and cut them away.

butterflying a chicken

TO BUTTERFLY A WHOLE CHICKEN is simply to remove its backbone. It's extremely easy to do, and the benefits are several: The bird roasts quicker, the breast is moister, more of the skin gets crispy, and it's easier to carve.

1 Position the chicken with the backbone facing up. Starting at the neck, use kitchen shears to cut through the ribs along one side of the backbone. Then cut down the other side of the backbone to remove it.

2 Turn the bird over and press on the breast with the heel of your hand to flatten it—you may feel a few bones crack, which is fine. Tuck the wing tips under the breast, if you want.

quick-roasting butterflied chicken with warm spice rub

By investing about three minutes up front to remove the backbone, you'll shave about fifteen minutes off the total roasting time. There's a back-of-the-throat kick to this Moroccan-inspired rub, but mostly it just makes you feel warm and cozy. *Pimentón dulce* is Spanish smoked sweet paprika, available in most specialty stores; if you can't find it, use sweet Hungarian paprika.

SERVES 4 AS A MAIN COURSE

1 teaspoon kosher salt, plus more for seasoning

1 teaspoon ground cumin

½ teaspoon ground coriander

½ teaspoon ground ginger

¼ teaspoon freshly ground black pepper

¼ teaspoon ground allspice

¼ teaspoon ground cayenne

¼ teaspoon ground cloves

¼ teaspoon *pimentón dulce*

¼ teaspoon sugar

1 (3½-pound) chicken

Lime wedges, for garnish

PREHEAT the oven to 425°F. In a small bowl, combine the 1 teaspoon salt, the spices, and sugar. Stir to blend.

REMOVE the giblets from the bird; discard or reserve for another use. Butterfly the chicken by removing the backbone with kitchen shears (see opposite page).

SEASON both sides of the chicken generously with salt, and rub all of the spice mixture into the skin. Set the bird, skin side up, on a heavy-duty rimmed baking sheet and tuck the wingtips underneath the breast. Push the legs as far away from the breast as they'll go.

ROAST the chicken until a meat thermometer inserted into the deepest part of the breast reads 165°F, 30 to 40 minutes (the thigh temperature will be higher; the breast cooks slower on a butterflied bird). If the spices look like they're on the verge of burning during the last 5 minutes, tent the chicken with aluminum foil. Transfer the chicken to a cutting board and let it rest for 10 minutes. Carve and serve with the lime wedges.

carving turkey

SOME PEOPLE REVEL IN THEIR ROLE AS TURKEY CARVER, but if it's your first time, the big bird can seem daunting. Don't worry, carving a turkey is doable for novices, and it's quite satisfying too. Before you start, set the turkey on a large carving board with a moat (or set the board inside a rimmed baking sheet). Also, sharpen your knife; a thin slicer is ideal, but sharpness is more important than blade type. A carving fork is helpful for stabilizing the turkey, but rather than piercing the bird with the tines (which releases its juices), just press the fork flat against the meat.

legs

1 Cut through the skin between the leg and body, and slice down to where the thigh attaches to the bird. Use your hand to forcefully bend the thigh away from the breast. Cut through the joint between the thigh and body to separate the leg.

2 Set the leg on the board, skin side up, and cut between the drumstick and thigh to separate them. Aim for the joint, which is a little closer to the drumstick than you might expect.

3 To carve the thigh, turn it skin side down and cut along both sides of the bone to release it from the meat. Pull out the bone. Turn the meat over so the skin side is up. Cut across the grain (perpendicular to where the bone had been) in thick slices. Repeat these steps with the other leg.

If you want to carve the drumstick, cut a slice or two off one side parallel to the bone. Rotate the leg and carve off another slice. Continue turning the drumstick until all sides are carved. The drumstick contains a few hard tendons, so be sure to remove them as you carve.

breast

To carve the breast meat, you have a couple of options. The more traditional method, often used for tableside carving, is to cut large sheets of meat off the breast. A more contemporary approach is to remove the breast in one piece and then slice it crosswise. The slices are smaller but they'll be moister and more tender because they're cut across the grain, plus each slice contains a generous portion of skin.

TRADITIONAL METHOD:

1 Stabilize the breast with the tines of a carving fork and make a deep horizontal cut into the bottom of the breast, as close to the wing as possible. This base cut lets the slices fall away from the bird more easily.

2 Starting at the top of the breast, carve thin slices parallel to the breastbone, ending at the base cut.

MODERN METHOD:

1 Turn the turkey so the wings are nearest you. Remove the entire breast by cutting down along one side of the breastbone. Work your way along the bone, gently pulling away the breast meat so you can see where to cut. When you hit the wishbone, follow it down to the wing. Cut the breast away from the carcass.

2 Set the breast on the board. Slice it across the grain, on the diagonal if you like.

wings

The wings help stabilize the bird, so remove them last. Cut into the joint where the wing attaches to the backbone. Cut off the wing tip (if you haven't already) and set the wing on the platter whole, or else separate the two segments by cutting through the joint.

trimming silverskin from tenderloin

BEEF, PORK, AND LAMB TENDERLOINS have a thin, shiny membrane known as silverskin that shrinks but doesn't break down at high temperatures; it should be trimmed to prevent the meat from curling during cooking. It may appear as one long wide swath, or it may only show up in patches. Use a sharp boning knife, a paring knife, or another knife with a thin, narrow blade.

1 Insert the tip of the knife under the silverskin, angling the blade a little upward toward the membrane. Cut between the meat and silverskin, holding the silverskin with your hand to keep it taut. When you get to the end of the silverskin, cut through to detach one side. Then reverse direction to remove the membrane on the other end. Continue in this way until all patches of silverskin are trimmed.

butterflying boneless meat and fish

BUTTERFLYING A BONELESS CUT OF MEAT transforms a thick or uneven piece into a thinner, larger one. You might do this to help the meat cook more evenly, or to allow you to spread on a stuffing and roll it up. Whether you're butterflying chicken breast, pork loin, beef tenderloin, or anything else, the strategy is the same. You'll make one or more horizontal cuts through the side of the meat to enable you to open it up, like a book. Butterflying large unevenly shaped cuts, such as leg of lamb, can be more complex; you'll need to approach the meat in sections.

1 Before you cut, decide how you want the flap to open; you usually want to cut into the thicker side and keep the "binding" on the thinner side. Position the blade so it's parallel to the board and slice the meat almost in half, stopping before cutting all the way through.

2 Open up the flap and press the new, larger piece of meat flat with your hand.

carving bone-in leg of lamb

A LEG OF LAMB CONSISTS OF SEVERAL MUSCLES, some more sinewy and others more tender, and the grain runs in different directions. Some people carve a bone-in leg by slicing parallel to the bone, and that works fine, but you'll get a little more tenderness if you cut perpendicular to the bone as shown here. To make carving easier, be sure the butcher has removed the hip and pelvic bone, or aitch bone, and ask that the shank bone stay on—it makes a convenient handle. Use a slicing knife or another knife with a narrow, thin blade.

1 Turn the leg so a meaty side faces up. Holding the shank bone with one hand or using a carving fork to stabilize the leg, cut several slices straight down toward the bone.

2 Turn the knife blade so it's parallel to the board and cut all the slices off the bone. Continue carving more slices as needed. When you've removed all the meat from one side, rotate the leg and carve the same way on the other sides.

roast leg of lamb with fennel seeds and rosemary crust

This is a delicious excuse to learn to carve bone-in leg of lamb. For an instant side dish, toss some potatoes around the lamb while it's roasting. When it's time to carve, start on the side with the crust. If some falls off as you slice, that's okay— just scoop it onto each serving.

SERVES 8 TO 10

2 cups fresh coarse bread crumbs

½ cup plus 2 tablespoons pine nuts

3 tablespoons coarsely chopped
fresh rosemary (see page 132)

4 anchovy fillets

3 medium cloves garlic

2 teaspoons fennel seeds, crushed
in a mortar or with a mallet

½ cup plus 3 tablespoons
extra-virgin olive oil

2 tablespoons Dijon mustard

Kosher salt

Freshly ground black pepper

6 pound bone-in leg of lamb (aitch
bone removed), shank bone on

PREHEAT the oven to 375°F. In a food processor, combine the bread crumbs, pine nuts, rosemary, anchovy, garlic, and fennel seeds. Process until the nuts and garlic are finely chopped, 10 to 15 seconds. Add ½ cup of the olive oil, mustard, a pinch of salt, and a few grinds of pepper to the food processor. Process until combined.

HEAT the remaining 3 tablespoons of oil in a large, heavy-duty roasting pan set over medium heat. Sear the lamb on all sides until deeply browned, 3 to 4 minutes per side. (You'll need to prop up and support the leg with tongs to sear some areas.)

SET the leg in the pan with the flatter side down. Spread the bread crumb mixture evenly on top of the leg and partially down the sides. Roast until medium rare, 70 to 80 minutes, when an instant-read thermometer inserted into the deepest section of meat (without touching the bone) should read 130°F. Let the meat rest for at least 20 minutes before carving (see opposite page).

carving standing rib roast

THE EASIEST WAY TO CARVE PRIME RIB is to cut the whole roast off the ribs and slice vertically. Use a sharpened slicing or carving knife (ideally an inch or two longer than the roast) and a carving fork to stabilize the meat.

1 Roll the roast so the ends of the bones point up. Holding the bones with one hand, cut downward, keeping the blade as close to the bones as you can, to remove the meat in one piece. If the butcher has not removed the chine bones, you'll need to cut around them at the bottom of the ribs.

2 Set the roast on the board with the fat side up. Stabilize the meat with a fork. Cut ¼- to ½-inch-thick slices.

tip TO CARVE BEAUTIFUL SLICES OF MEAT WITHOUT KNIFE MARKS, take long, smooth strokes with the knife, pulling the knife toward you rather than sawing back and forth. A slicing knife will help but if you don't have one, use the longest, sharpest knife you have.

cutting across the grain

THE NEXT TIME YOU FIND YOURSELF standing in front of an expensive steak or roast with no clue how to carve it, just remember this: cutting across the grain gives you more tender slices. But how do you find the grain? Examine the meat and you'll see that the fibers all run in one direction (unless you have a cut with multiple muscles, in which case the grain may run in more than one direction). You want to position the knife so you're cutting perpendicular to these fibers, not parallel to them.

TABLESIDE CARVING can add a little ceremonial drama to your meal, but if you carve in the kitchen, you'll feel more in control and avoid performance anxiety. Wherever you carve, you'll be more successful if you've set up properly before you start.

AFTER COOKING, tent the meat with foil and let the it rest for 10 to 30 minutes (depending on its size) so the juices can redistribute.

SET THE MEAT on a nice large carving  board with a moat to catch the juices. If you don't have one, set a large cutting board inside a rimmed baking sheet.

BE SURE TO HONE if not sharpen your carving knife. It will make the carving easier, and you'll get cleaner slices.

HAVE A PLATTER or individual plates ready to receive the meat. For an extra touch, warm the plates in the oven at low temperature (wrap them in a towel to retain the heat).

CARVE ONLY what you need for the meal. An uncut portion of meat retains its juices better than slices.

filleting and skinning fish

WHY WOULD YOU NEED TO FILLET A FISH YOURSELF? To be honest, you probably wouldn't. Any fishmonger will gladly do it for you, and do it better. But if you're ready for a challenge, you might want to give it a whirl. Sharpen your fillet knife, or your thinnest, most flexible blade. This method works on salmon, snapper, cod, bluefish, or any other similar roundfish; just be sure the fish is scaled and cleaned before you start. And don't toss the head and scraps; they'll make a rich seafood broth for your next bouillabaisse or paella.

1 If the fins have not been removed, cut them off with kitchen shears. Set the scaled and cleaned fish on a board with the backbone toward you. (If you're right-handed, the head should be on the right side.) Position a fillet knife a little behind the gills, tilt the blade so you're cutting toward the head, and cut straight down to the backbone.

2 When you reach the backbone, turn the blade so it's parallel to the board and you're cutting toward the tail. Hold the top of the fish securely with your hand as you cut toward the tail (use a paper towel if the fish is slippery). Try to keep the blade as close to the bones as you can for maximum yield. If the knife is extremely sharp, you can push it cleanly through the flesh. If pushing doesn't work, use long, sweeping strokes and avoid sawing back and forth, which roughs up the fillet.

3 When you get to the tail, cut through the skin. Remove the fillet carefully, turn the fish over, and fillet the other side the same way, keeping the backbone toward you.

4 If there are bones along the bottom of the fillet, trim them off along with the belly flap. If there is a tiny edge of bones along the fin side of the fillet, cut them off.

5 Feel for pin bones by running your fingertips on top of the fillet in the direction of the tail. Pull them out using tweezers or needle-nose pliers, pulling in the same direction that they're pointing to avoid tearing the flesh.

6 If you need to skin the fillet, set it close to the edge of the board, skin side down, to give your hand clearance as you cut. Hold the tail (use a paper towel if it's slippery) with one hand and cut between the flesh and the skin. Keep the cutting edge angled slightly toward the skin, and use a very slight sawing motion. As you cut, grab more of the skin and pull it taut.

lemon-dill gravlax

To make this Scandinavian specialty, you rub raw salmon with salt, dill, and other flavorings and cure it in the fridge. The process takes three days, at which point you'll have smooth, silky cured salmon, which makes an impressive appetizer served with baguette toasts or black bread and a swirl of crème fraîche. The twist in this recipe is the layer of sliced lemon, which infuses the fish and brings out a light, delicate flavor. This calls for a whole salmon so you can try your hand at filleting, if you want, and it makes enough for a large party, plus leftovers. For smaller gatherings, use one side of salmon, or even a one-pound center-cut fillet; wrap the plastic directly over the salt cure (and use less of it).

SERVES 16 TO 20 AS AN APPETIZER

1 lemon

1 cup kosher salt

¾ cup sugar

1 teaspoon coarsely ground white or black pepper, or a combination

1 very fresh whole salmon, about 8 pounds, filleted but not skinned (to yield 2 fillets, 5½ pounds total) (see page 175)

3 tablespoons dry gin

1 large bunch dill, ends trimmed, leaves and stems chopped coarsely (2½ cups)

ZEST the lemon to yield ½ teaspoon of loosely packed grated zest. Put the zest in a medium bowl. Cut the lemon into ⅛-inch-thick slices and reserve. Add the salt, sugar, and pepper to the bowl with the zest. Mix well and set aside.

COVER a large baking sheet with a few long sheets of plastic wrap, letting the edges hang over the sides. Set the 2 salmon fillets skin side down on the sheet. Sprinkle the salt cure over both fillets and rub it in evenly. Arrange the lemon slices evenly on one side of salmon. Drizzle the gin over the lemon. Distribute the dill on top.

PUT the other fillet on top, flesh side down. Wrap the plastic tightly around the fish, using more plastic if necessary to completely encase it. Set another large baking sheet on top of the salmon and weight it with several small cans of food (or any heavy objects in your refrigerator). Refrigerate for 3 days.

POUR off the brine that has seeped from the salmon. Unwrap the fish and use your hands to brush off and discard the salt cure, lemon, and most of the dill. Using a salmon slicer or another very sharp, long, narrow knife, cut very thin, almost translucent slices on the diagonal, using long, smooth strokes. If you can see the knife blade through the salmon as you slice, you're doing well. Cover and store leftover gravlax in the refrigerator for up to 5 days.

Index